Ivan Kushnir

Economy of Ukraine

Series "Economy in countries"

first published: 2019
last updated: 2021-01-26

Ivan Kushnir. Economy of Ukraine. Series "Economy in countries". - 2019. - 55 pages.

This book about the economy of Ukraine from the 1990s to the 2010s. Source data from UN Data.

Size. In the 2010s, the GDP of Ukraine was equal to $137.3 billion per year; the value of agriculture was $12.7 billion; the value of industry was $28.9 billion. Since the share in the world is between .1% and 1%, the country is classified as an average economy.

Productivity. In the 2010s, the GDP per capita was $3 053.7, the value of agriculture per capita was $283.3, the value of industry per capita was $642.8. Since the productivity is less the average below average, the economy is classified as least developed.

Growth. In the 2010s, the growth of gross domestic product was 0.012%; the growth of agriculture was 3.4%; the growth of industry was -2.6%.

Structure. In the 2010s, the economy of Ukraine included: services (32.6%), industry (24.4%), trade (17.1%), transportation (12.1%), agriculture (10.8%), and construction (3.0%).

Exports and imports. In the 2010s, the imports were 14.6% higher than the exports, the net imports were equal to 6.8% of the GDP. The technological structure of exports are not better than the structure of imports.

Consumption and reproduction. The attitude of reproduction to the consumption is not better than the global average, so the share of GDP in the world will not increase.

Series "Economy in countries": parallel.page.link/en

© Ivan Kushnir, 2019

All rights reserved.

ISBN: 9781795121606

Contents

Part I. Size	4
Chapter I. Gross domestic product	5
Chapter II. Value added	8
Chapter III. Gross national income	11
Part II. Structure	14
Chapter IV. Agriculture	15
Chapter V. Industry	18
Chapter 5.1. Manufacturing	21
Chapter VI. Construction	24
Chapter VII. Transportation	27
Chapter VIII. Trade	30
Chapter IX. Services	33
Part III. External relations	36
Chapter X. Exports	37
Chapter XI. Imports	40
Part IV. Consumption	43
Chapter XII. Government consumption expenditure	44
Chapter XIII. Household consumption expenditure	47
Chapter XIV. Food consumption	50
Part V. Reproduction	52
Chapter XV. Gross fixed capital formation	53

Part I. Size

	The 2010s
GDP	$137.3 billion
The share in the world	0.18%
Share in Europe	0.65%
Share in Eastern Europe	4.3%

Chapter I. Gross domestic product

The GDP of Ukraine grew from $61.5 billion per year in the 1990s to $137.3 billion per year in the 2010s, that is by $75.8 billion or 2.2 times. The change occurred at $74.4 billion due to a 2.2-fold increase in prices, as also at $8.4 billion due to a 1.2-fold increase in productivity, as well as at -$7.0 billion due to the decline in population. The average annual growth in GDP is -1.6%. The minimum value of GDP was in 2000 at $32.4 billion. The maximum value of GDP was in 2008 at $188.1 billion.

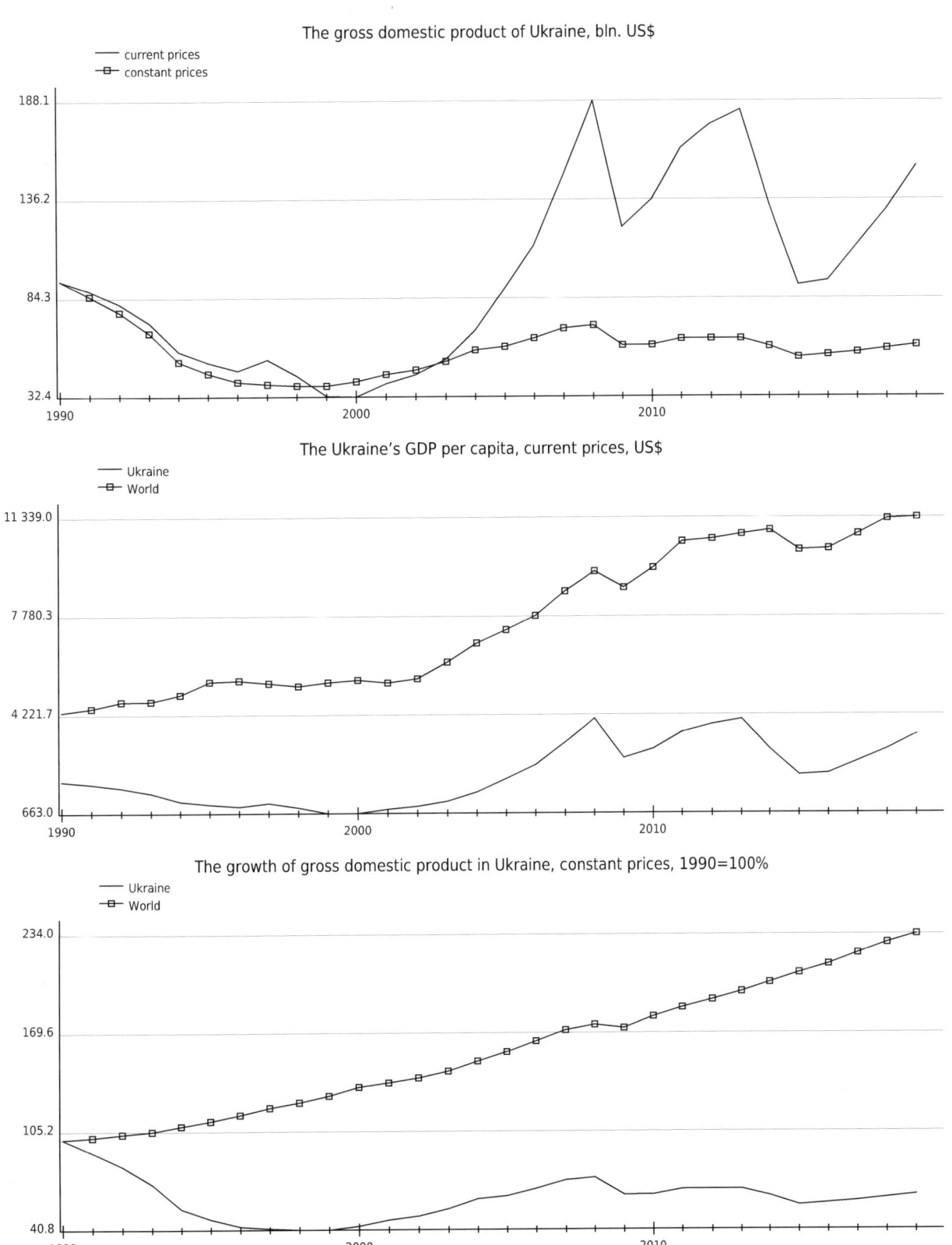

The 1990s

The Ukrainian GDP was $61.5 billion per year in the 1990s, ranked 46th in the world, and was on a par with Egypt ($62.8 billion). The share in the world was 0.21%, and 0.63% in Europe.

The GDP of Ukraine consisted of: household consumption expenditure (54.2%), capital formation (28.2%), and government consumption expenditure (18.2%).

The Ukraine's gross domestic product per capita was $1 211.6 in the 1990s, ranked 127th in the world, and was on a par with Palestine ($1 200.4), Guyana ($1 189.7), South-Eastern Asia ($1 187.4). The GDP per capita in Ukraine was less than GDP per capita in the world ($5 020.1) in 4.1 times, and was less than GDP per capita in Europe ($13 469.1) in 11.1 times.

The growth of GDP in Ukraine was -9.5% in the 1990s, ranked 204th in the world. The growth of gross domestic product in Ukraine (-9.5%) was less than growth of GDP in the world (2.8%), was less than growth of gross domestic product in Europe (1.4%).

Comparison with neighbors. The Ukrainian GDP was greater than in Hungary ($43.2 billion), in Romania ($34.1 billion), in Belarus ($16.3 billion), in Bulgaria ($13.2 billion), and in Moldova ($2.7 billion); but less than in Russia ($417.8 billion) and in Poland ($126.0 billion). The GDP per capita in Ukraine was greater than in Moldova ($618.9); but less than in Hungary ($4.2 thousand), in Poland ($3.3 thousand), in Russia ($2.8 thousand), in Belarus ($1 617.3), in Bulgaria ($1 569.2), and in Romania ($1 482.1). The growth of gross domestic product in Ukraine was greater than in Moldova (-11.3%); but less than in Poland (2.0%), in Hungary (-0.55%), in Belarus (-2.0%), in Romania (-2.0%), in Bulgaria (-3.5%), and in Russia (-5.3%).

Comparison with leaders. The GDP of Ukraine was less than in the United States ($7.6 trillion), in Japan ($4.3 trillion), in Germany ($2.2 trillion), in France ($1.4 trillion), and in the United Kingdom ($1.3 trillion). The Ukrainian gross domestic product per capita was less than in Japan ($34.3 thousand), in the United States ($28.7 thousand), in Germany ($27.0 thousand), in France ($24.1 thousand), and in the United Kingdom ($22.9 thousand). The growth of GDP in Ukraine was less than in the USA (3.2%), in the United Kingdom (2.3%), in Germany (2.2%), in France (2.0%), and in Japan (1.5%).

The 2000s

The gross domestic product of Ukraine was $89.4 billion per year in the 2000s, ranked 52nd in the world. The share in the world was 0.19%, and 0.58% in Europe.

The gross domestic product of Ukraine included: household expenditure (60.6%), capital formation (23.5%), and government expenditure (17.7%).

The Ukrainian gross domestic product per capita was $1 894.9 in the 2000s, ranked 140th in the world, and was on a par with Armenia ($1 915.3). The gross domestic product per capita in Ukraine was less than GDP per capita in the world ($7 176.3) in 3.8 times, and was less than gross domestic product per capita in Europe ($21 115.4) in 11.1 times.

The growth of gross domestic product in Ukraine was 4.5% in the 2000s, ranked 76th in the world, and was on a par with the Maldives (4.5%), Pakistan (4.5%), Slovakia (4.5%). The growth of gross domestic product in Ukraine (4.5%) was greater than growth of GDP in the world (3.0%), was greater than growth of GDP in Europe (1.8%).

Comparison with neighbors. The Ukrainian gross domestic product was greater than in Belarus ($31.1 billion), in Bulgaria ($30.6 billion), and in Moldova ($3.8 billion); but less than in Russia ($794.5 billion), in Poland ($308.8 billion), in Romania ($104.4 billion), and in Hungary ($101.5 billion). The gross domestic product per capita in Ukraine was greater than in Moldova ($903.9); but less than in Hungary ($10.1 thousand), in Poland ($8.0 thousand), in Russia ($5.5 thousand), in Romania ($4.9 thousand), in Bulgaria ($4.0 thousand), and in Belarus ($3.2 thousand). The growth of GDP in Ukraine was greater than in Poland (4.0%) and in Hungary (2.4%); but less than in Belarus (7.2%), in Russia (5.4%), in Romania (4.9%), in Bulgaria (4.9%), and in Moldova (4.6%).

Comparison with leaders. The gross domestic product of Ukraine was less than in the United States ($12.6 trillion), in Japan ($4.7 trillion), in Germany ($2.8 trillion), in China ($2.6 trillion), and in the United Kingdom ($2.3 trillion). The Ukrainian gross domestic product per capita was less than in the United States ($42.8 thousand), in the United Kingdom ($38.4 thousand), in Japan ($36.4 thousand), in Germany ($34.0 thousand), and in China ($1 954.1). The growth of gross domestic product in Ukraine was greater than in the United States (1.9%), in the United Kingdom (1.7%), in Germany (0.73%), and in Japan (0.50%); but less than in China (10.3%).

The 2010s

Chapter I. Gross domestic product

The gross domestic product of Ukraine was $137.3 billion per year in the 2010s, ranked 59th in the world, and was on a par with Hungary ($139.9 billion), Kuwait ($140.0 billion). The share in the world was 0.18%, and 0.65% in Europe.

The GDP of Ukraine included: household consumption expenditure (69.1%), public expenditure (19.1%), and capital formation (18.6%).

The GDP per capita in Ukraine was $3 053.7 in the 2010s, ranked 144th in the world, and was on a par with Vanuatu ($3.0 thousand), Morocco ($3.1 thousand), Palestine ($3.1 thousand). The GDP per capita in Ukraine was less than GDP per capita in the world ($10 603.1) in 3.5 times, and was less than gross domestic product per capita in Europe ($28 186.8) in 9.2 times.

The growth of GDP in Ukraine was 0% in the 2010s, ranked 193rd in the world. The growth of gross domestic product in Ukraine (0.012%) was less than growth of GDP in the world (3.1%), was less than growth of gross domestic product in Europe (1.6%).

Comparison with neighbors. The GDP of Ukraine was 2.2 times higher than in Belarus ($62.1 billion), 2.4 times higher than in Bulgaria ($57.2 billion), and 14.9 times higher than in Moldova ($9.2 billion); but 12.9 times lower than in Russia ($1.8 trillion), 3.8 times lower than in Poland ($523.0 billion), 30.7% lower than in Romania ($198.1 billion), and 1.8% lower than in Hungary ($139.9 billion). The GDP per capita in Ukraine was 35.0% higher than in Moldova ($2.3 thousand); but 4.7 times lower than in Hungary ($14.3 thousand), 4.5 times lower than in Poland ($13.7 thousand), 4.0 times lower than in Russia ($12.3 thousand), 3.3 times lower than in Romania ($9.9 thousand), 2.6 times lower than in Bulgaria ($7.9 thousand), and 2.2 times lower than in Belarus ($6.6 thousand). The growth of gross domestic product in Ukraine was less than in Moldova (4.3%), in Poland (3.6%), in Romania (3.1%), in Hungary (2.8%), in Bulgaria (2.3%), in Russia (1.9%), and in Belarus (1.8%).

Comparison with leaders. The GDP of Ukraine was 130.8 times lower than in the USA ($18.0 trillion), 76.5 times lower than in China ($10.5 trillion), 38.1 times lower than in Japan ($5.2 trillion), 26.7 times lower than in Germany ($3.7 trillion), and 20.2 times lower than in the United Kingdom ($2.8 trillion). The gross domestic product per capita in Ukraine was 18.4 times lower than in the United States ($56.2 thousand), 14.6 times lower than in Germany ($44.7 thousand), 13.8 times lower than in the United Kingdom ($42.2 thousand), 13.4 times lower than in Japan ($40.9 thousand), and 2.5 times lower than in China ($7.5 thousand). The growth of gross domestic product in Ukraine was less than in China (7.7%), in the USA (2.3%), in Germany (1.9%), in the United Kingdom (1.8%), and in Japan (1.3%).

Chapter II. Value added

The Ukraine's value added grew up from $59.8 billion per year in the 1990s to $118.4 billion per year in the 2010s, that is by $58.6 billion or 98.1%. The change occurred at $56.6 billion due to a 1.9-fold increase in prices, as also at $8.9 billion due to a 1.2-fold increase in productivity, as well as at -$6.8 billion due to the decline in population. The average annual growth in value added is -1.8%. The minimum value of value added was in 1999 at $27.2 billion. The maximum value of value added was in 2008 at $164.6 billion.

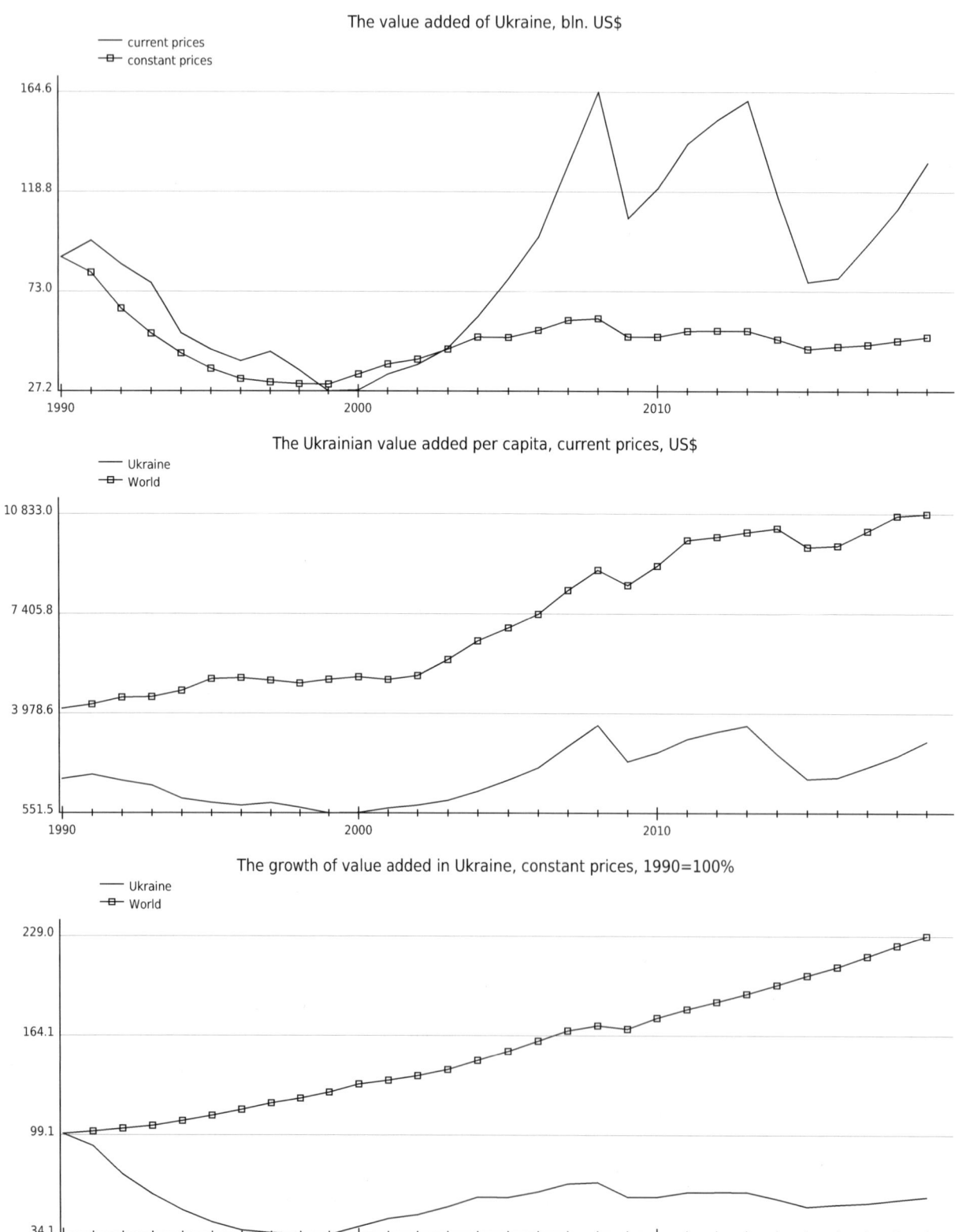

Chapter II. Value added

The 1990s

The value added of Ukraine was $59.8 billion per year in the 1990s, ranked 44th in the world, and was on a par with Egypt ($59.3 billion). The share in the world was 0.22%, and 0.67% in Europe.

The total value added of Ukraine consisted of: industry (35.9%), services (20.5%), agriculture (18.3%), transportation (10.3%), trade (7.5%), and construction (7.5%).

The Ukrainian value added per capita was $1 177.9 in the 1990s, ranked 127th in the world, and was on a par with South-Eastern Asia ($1 185.5), Congo ($1 159.8), Tuvalu ($1 155.3). The Ukraine's value added per capita was less than value added per capita in the world ($4 799.9) in 4.1 times, and was less than value added per capita in Europe ($12 269.4) in 10.4 times.

The growth of value added in Ukraine was -11.3% in the 1990s, ranked 206th in the world. The growth of value added in Ukraine (-11.3%) was less than growth of value added in the world (2.7%), was less than growth of value added in Europe (1.3%).

Comparison with neighbors. The value added of Ukraine was greater than in Hungary ($37.3 billion), in Romania ($31.7 billion), in Belarus ($14.9 billion), in Bulgaria ($12.2 billion), and in Moldova ($2.5 billion); but less than in Russia ($392.4 billion) and in Poland ($113.3 billion). The Ukrainian value added per capita was greater than in Moldova ($579.0); but less than in Hungary ($3.6 thousand), in Poland ($3.0 thousand), in Russia ($2.7 thousand), in Belarus ($1 479.7), in Bulgaria ($1 447.3), and in Romania ($1 377.0). The growth of value added in Ukraine was greater than in Moldova (-11.6%); but less than in Poland (2.2%), in Hungary (-0.18%), in Romania (-0.94%), in Belarus (-3.7%), in Bulgaria (-3.9%), and in Russia (-4.8%).

Comparison with leaders. The Ukraine's value added was less than in the United States ($7.6 trillion), in Japan ($4.3 trillion), in Germany ($2.0 trillion), in France ($1.3 trillion), and in the United Kingdom ($1.2 trillion). The Ukraine's value added per capita was less than in Japan ($34.2 thousand), in the United States ($28.6 thousand), in Germany ($24.5 thousand), in France ($21.6 thousand), and in the UK ($21.4 thousand). The growth of value added in Ukraine was less than in the United States (2.8%), in the UK (2.4%), in Germany (2.1%), in France (1.8%), and in Japan (1.8%).

The 2000s

The value added of Ukraine was $79.0 billion per year in the 2000s, ranked 54th in the world, and was on a par with Kuwait ($79.9 billion), Puerto Rico ($80.7 billion). The share in the world was 0.18%, and 0.57% in Europe.

The total value added of Ukraine consisted of: services (30.3%), industry (28.8%), trade (14.8%), transportation (12.6%), agriculture (9.4%), and construction (4.2%).

The Ukraine's value added per capita was $1 673.3 in the 2000s, ranked 142nd in the world, and was on a par with Central Asia ($1 675.9), Syria ($1 712.8), Armenia ($1 715.8). The value added per capita in Ukraine was less than value added per capita in the world ($6 818.0) in 4.1 times, and was less than value added per capita in Europe ($18 944.1) in 11.3 times.

The growth of value added in Ukraine was 5.6% in the 2000s, ranked 36th in the world, and was on a par with Suriname (5.5%), Cuba (5.6%), Southern Asia (5.6%). The growth of value added in Ukraine (5.6%) was greater than growth of value added in the world (2.9%), was greater than growth of value added in Europe (1.7%).

Comparison with neighbors. The value added of Ukraine was greater than in Belarus ($26.5 billion), in Bulgaria ($26.3 billion), and in Moldova ($3.3 billion); but less than in Russia ($685.9 billion), in Poland ($271.7 billion), in Romania ($93.3 billion), and in Hungary ($87.1 billion). The Ukraine's value added per capita was greater than in Moldova ($789.7); but less than in Hungary ($8.6 thousand), in Poland ($7.1 thousand), in Russia ($4.8 thousand), in Romania ($4.4 thousand), in Bulgaria ($3.4 thousand), and in Belarus ($2.8 thousand). The growth of value added in Ukraine was greater than in Russia (5.0%), in Romania (4.7%), in Bulgaria (4.7%), in Poland (3.6%), in Moldova (3.2%), and in Hungary (2.2%); but less than in Belarus (6.2%).

Comparison with leaders. The value added of Ukraine was less than in the United States ($12.6 trillion), in Japan ($4.7 trillion), in China ($2.6 trillion), in Germany ($2.5 trillion), and in the UK ($2.1 trillion). The Ukrainian value added per capita was less than in the USA ($42.8 thousand), in Japan ($36.4 thousand), in the UK ($34.6 thousand), in Germany ($30.7 thousand), and in China ($1 954.1). The growth of value added in Ukraine was greater than in the United States (1.7%), in the United Kingdom (1.7%), in Germany (0.65%), and in Japan (0.27%); but less than in China (10.2%).

The 2010s

The value added of Ukraine was $118.4 billion per year in the 2010s, ranked 58th in the world, and was on a par with Hungary ($118.3 billion). The share in the world was 0.16%, and 0.63% in Europe.

The total value added of Ukraine consisted of: services (32.6%), industry (24.4%), trade (17.1%), transportation (12.1%), agriculture (10.8%), and construction (3.0%).

The value added per capita in Ukraine was $2 634.2 in the 2010s, ranked 149th in the world, and was on a par with Bhutan ($2.7 thousand), Palestine ($2.7 thousand). The value added per capita in Ukraine was less than value added per capita in the world ($10 094.6) in 3.8 times, and was less than value added per capita in Europe ($25 251.2) in 9.6 times.

The growth of value added in Ukraine was -0% in the 2010s, ranked 192nd in the world. The growth of value added in Ukraine (-0.011%) was less than growth of value added in the world (3.1%), was less than growth of value added in Europe (1.6%).

Comparison with neighbors. The Ukrainian value added was 0.15% higher than in Hungary ($118.3 billion), 2.2 times higher than in Belarus ($54.2 billion), 2.4 times higher than in Bulgaria ($49.6 billion), and 14.9 times higher than in Moldova ($8.0 billion); but 13.2 times lower than in Russia ($1.6 trillion), 3.9 times lower than in Poland ($461.3 billion), and 33.0% lower than in Romania ($176.7 billion). The Ukraine's value added per capita was 34.5% higher than in Moldova ($1 958.0); but 4.6 times lower than in Poland ($12.1 thousand), 4.6 times lower than in Hungary ($12.1 thousand), 4.1 times lower than in Russia ($10.8 thousand), 3.4 times lower than in Romania ($8.9 thousand), 2.6 times lower than in Bulgaria ($6.9 thousand), and 2.2 times lower than in Belarus ($5.7 thousand). The growth of value added in Ukraine was less than in Moldova (4.7%), in Hungary (3.7%), in Poland (3.6%), in Romania (3.0%), in Belarus (1.7%), in Russia (1.7%), and in Bulgaria (1.6%).

Comparison with leaders. The Ukraine's value added was 151.7 times lower than in the United States ($18.0 trillion), 88.7 times lower than in China ($10.5 trillion), 43.9 times lower than in Japan ($5.2 trillion), 27.9 times lower than in Germany ($3.3 trillion), and 20.9 times lower than in the UK ($2.5 trillion). The Ukraine's value added per capita was 21.3 times lower than in the USA ($56.2 thousand), 15.4 times lower than in Japan ($40.7 thousand), 15.3 times lower than in Germany ($40.3 thousand), 14.3 times lower than in the United Kingdom ($37.7 thousand), and 2.8 times lower than in China ($7.5 thousand). The growth of value added in Ukraine was less than in China (7.7%), in the USA (2.2%), in Germany (1.9%), in the UK (1.8%), and in Japan (1.3%).

Chapter III. Gross national income

The Ukrainian GNI rose from $59.2 billion per year in the 1990s to $139.0 billion per year in the 2010s, that is by $79.8 billion or 2.3 times. The change occurred at $75.4 billion due to a 2.2-fold increase in prices, as also at $11.2 billion due to a 1.2-fold increase in productivity, as well as at -$6.8 billion due to the drop in population. The average annual growth in GNI is -1.4%. The minimum value of GNI was in 2000 at $30.3 billion. The maximum value of gross national income was in 2013 at $187.7 billion.

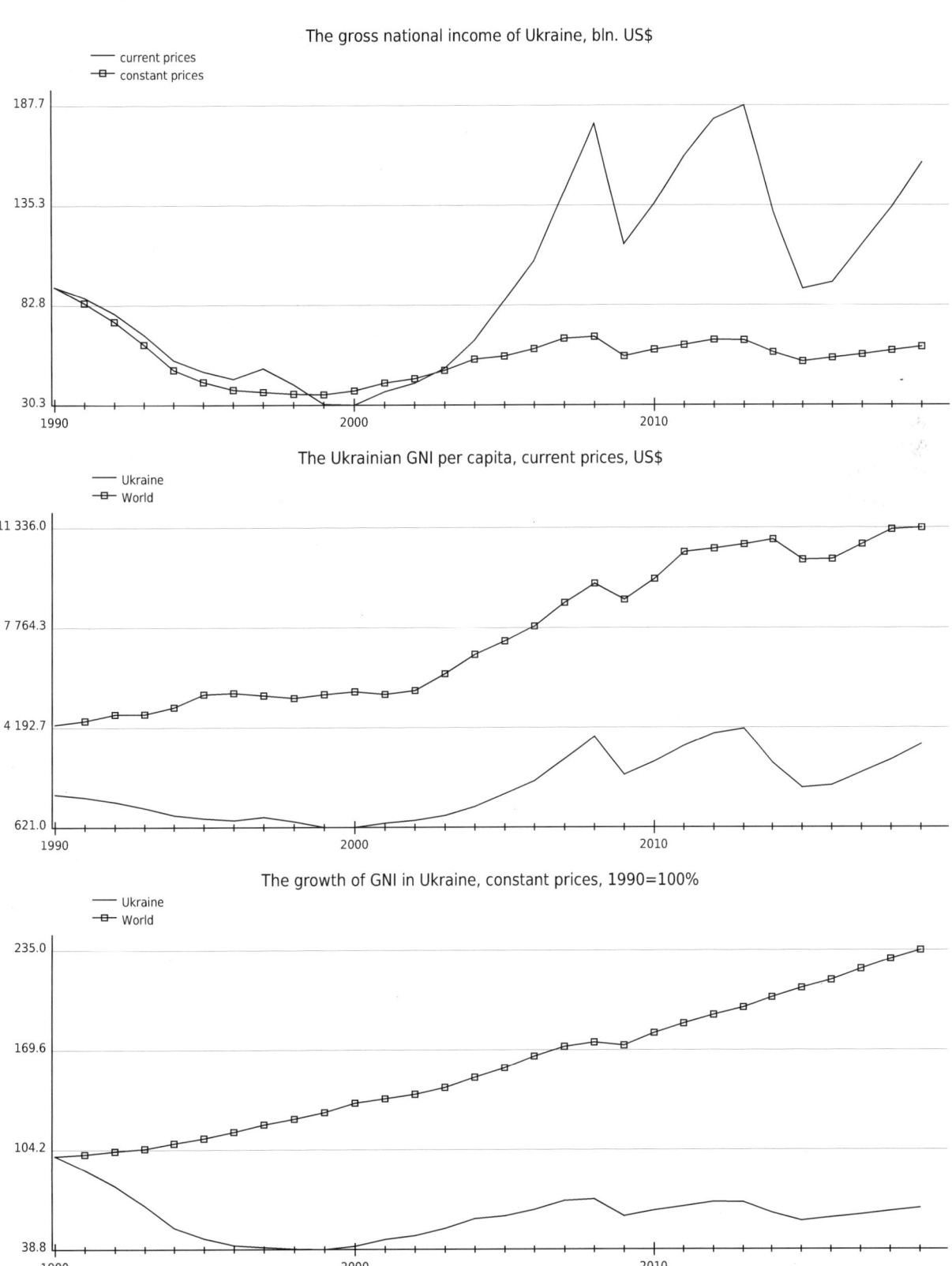

The 1990s

The Ukraine's gross national income was $59.2 billion per year in the 1990s, ranked 46th in the world. The share in the world was 0.21%, and 0.61% in Europe.

The gross national income per capita in Ukraine was $1 165.8 in the 1990s, ranked 129th in the world, and was on a par with South-Eastern Asia ($1 167.8), Guatemala ($1 159.6), Samoa ($1 192.1). The Ukraine's GNI per capita was less than gross national income per capita in the world ($4 991.4) in 4.3 times, and was less than GNI per capita in Europe ($13 437.3) in 11.5 times.

The growth of gross national income in Ukraine was -10% in the 1990s, ranked 204th in the world, and was on a par with Montserrat (-10.0%), Georgia (-9.9%). The growth of GNI in Ukraine (-10.0%) was less than growth of gross national income in the world (2.8%), was less than growth of gross national income in Europe (1.3%).

Comparison with neighbors. The Ukraine's gross national income was greater than in Hungary ($41.1 billion), in Romania ($33.7 billion), in Belarus ($16.3 billion), in Bulgaria ($12.1 billion), and in Moldova ($2.7 billion); but less than in Russia ($411.1 billion) and in Poland ($122.1 billion). The gross national income per capita in Ukraine was greater than in Moldova ($622.8); but less than in Hungary ($4.0 thousand), in Poland ($3.2 thousand), in Russia ($2.8 thousand), in Belarus ($1 618.2), in Romania ($1 466.7), and in Bulgaria ($1 428.8). The growth of gross national income in Ukraine was greater than in Moldova (-11.0%); but less than in Poland (2.2%), in Hungary (-0.73%), in Belarus (-1.9%), in Romania (-2.2%), in Bulgaria (-3.4%), and in Russia (-5.7%).

Comparison with leaders. The Ukrainian gross national income was less than in the United States ($7.5 trillion), in Japan ($4.4 trillion), in Germany ($2.2 trillion), in France ($1.4 trillion), and in the UK ($1.3 trillion). The gross national income per capita in Ukraine was less than in Japan ($34.7 thousand), in the USA ($28.5 thousand), in Germany ($27.0 thousand), in France ($24.3 thousand), and in the United Kingdom ($23.0 thousand). The growth of gross national income in Ukraine was less than in the United States (3.4%), in France (2.2%), in the UK (2.0%), in Germany (2.0%), and in Japan (1.5%).

The 2000s

The gross national income of Ukraine was $85.0 billion per year in the 2000s, ranked 52nd in the world, and was on a par with Kuwait ($84.5 billion). The share in the world was 0.18%, and 0.55% in Europe.

The Ukrainian GNI per capita was $1 800.1 in the 2000s, ranked 139th in the world, and was on a par with South-Eastern Asia ($1 795.5), Angola ($1 780.2). The Ukraine's gross national income per capita was less than GNI per capita in the world ($7 165.2) in 4.0 times, and was less than GNI per capita in Europe ($21 073.1) in 11.7 times.

The growth of gross national income in Ukraine was 4.6% in the 2000s, ranked 78th in the world, and was on a par with Honduras (4.5%), Peru (4.6%). The growth of gross national income in Ukraine (4.6%) was greater than growth of GNI in the world (3.0%), was greater than growth of gross national income in Europe (1.8%).

Comparison with neighbors. The Ukraine's gross national income was greater than in Belarus ($30.9 billion), in Bulgaria ($29.9 billion), and in Moldova ($4.1 billion); but less than in Russia ($771.8 billion), in Poland ($302.5 billion), in Romania ($101.9 billion), and in Hungary ($95.3 billion). The Ukrainian GNI per capita was greater than in Moldova ($991.8); but less than in Hungary ($9.4 thousand), in Poland ($7.9 thousand), in Russia ($5.3 thousand), in Romania ($4.8 thousand), in Bulgaria ($3.9 thousand), and in Belarus ($3.2 thousand). The growth of GNI in Ukraine was greater than in Poland (3.8%) and in Hungary (2.7%); but less than in Belarus (6.9%), in Russia (5.5%), in Romania (5.0%), in Moldova (4.9%), and in Bulgaria (4.9%).

Comparison with leaders. The GNI of Ukraine was less than in the USA ($12.7 trillion), in Japan ($4.8 trillion), in Germany ($2.8 trillion), in China ($2.6 trillion), and in the United Kingdom ($2.3 trillion). The Ukraine's GNI per capita was less than in the USA ($43.2 thousand), in the UK ($38.5 thousand), in Japan ($37.1 thousand), in Germany ($34.2 thousand), and in China ($1 950.5). The growth of gross national income in Ukraine was greater than in the United States (1.8%), in the United Kingdom (1.7%), in Germany (1.0%), and in Japan (0.62%); but less than in China (10.4%).

The 2010s

The gross national income of Ukraine was $139.0 billion per year in the 2010s, ranked 58th in the world. The share in the world was 0.18%, and 0.66% in Europe.

The Ukraine's gross national income per capita was $3 092.0 in the 2010s, ranked 144th in the world, and was on a par with Morocco ($3.0 thousand), Northern Africa ($3.2 thousand). The Ukraine's gross national income per capita was less than gross national income

Chapter III. Gross national income

per capita in the world ($10 611.7) in 3.4 times, and was less than GNI per capita in Europe ($28 141.7) in 9.1 times.

The growth of gross national income in Ukraine was 0.8% in the 2010s, ranked 181st in the world, and was on a par with Saint Vincent and the Grenadines (0.84%). The growth of gross national income in Ukraine (0.84%) was less than growth of gross national income in the world (3.1%), was less than growth of gross national income in Europe (1.6%).

Comparison with neighbors. The gross national income of Ukraine was 3.3% higher than in Hungary ($134.6 billion), 2.3 times higher than in Belarus ($60.2 billion), 2.5 times higher than in Bulgaria ($56.3 billion), and 14.0 times higher than in Moldova ($9.9 billion); but 12.4 times lower than in Russia ($1.7 trillion), 3.6 times lower than in Poland ($503.4 billion), and 28.7% lower than in Romania ($195.0 billion). The GNI per capita in Ukraine was 27.0% higher than in Moldova ($2.4 thousand); but 4.4 times lower than in Hungary ($13.7 thousand), 4.3 times lower than in Poland ($13.2 thousand), 3.8 times lower than in Russia ($11.9 thousand), 3.2 times lower than in Romania ($9.8 thousand), 2.5 times lower than in Bulgaria ($7.8 thousand), and 2.1 times lower than in Belarus ($6.4 thousand). The growth of gross national income in Ukraine was less than in Moldova (4.2%), in Poland (3.5%), in Romania (3.0%), in Hungary (3.0%), in Bulgaria (2.6%), in Russia (1.9%), and in Belarus (1.7%).

Comparison with leaders. The GNI of Ukraine was 131.7 times lower than in the USA ($18.3 trillion), 75.3 times lower than in China ($10.5 trillion), 38.8 times lower than in Japan ($5.4 trillion), 27.0 times lower than in Germany ($3.7 trillion), and 19.8 times lower than in France ($2.7 trillion). The Ukraine's gross national income per capita was 18.5 times lower than in the United States ($57.3 thousand), 14.8 times lower than in Germany ($45.8 thousand), 13.6 times lower than in Japan ($42.2 thousand), 13.4 times lower than in France ($41.4 thousand), and 2.4 times lower than in China ($7.5 thousand). The growth of gross national income in Ukraine was less than in China (7.7%), in the USA (2.5%), in Germany (2.0%), in Japan (1.4%), and in France (1.4%).

Part II. Structure

	The 2010s
agriculture	10.8%
industry	24.4%
construction	3.0%
trade	17.1%
transportation	12.1%
services	32.6%

Chapter IV. Agriculture

Agriculture, hunting, forestry, fishing (ISIC A-B)

The agriculture of Ukraine rose from $10.9 billion per year in the 1990s to $12.7 billion per year in the 2010s, that is by $1.8 billion or 16.6%. The change occurred at -$1.9 billion due to a 1.1-fold decrease in prices, as also at $4.9 billion due to a 1.5-fold increase in productivity, as well as at -$1.2 billion due to the falling in population. The average annual growth in agriculture is 0.19%. The maximum value of agriculture was in 1990 at $22.0 billion. The minimum value of agriculture was in 1999 at $3.7 billion.

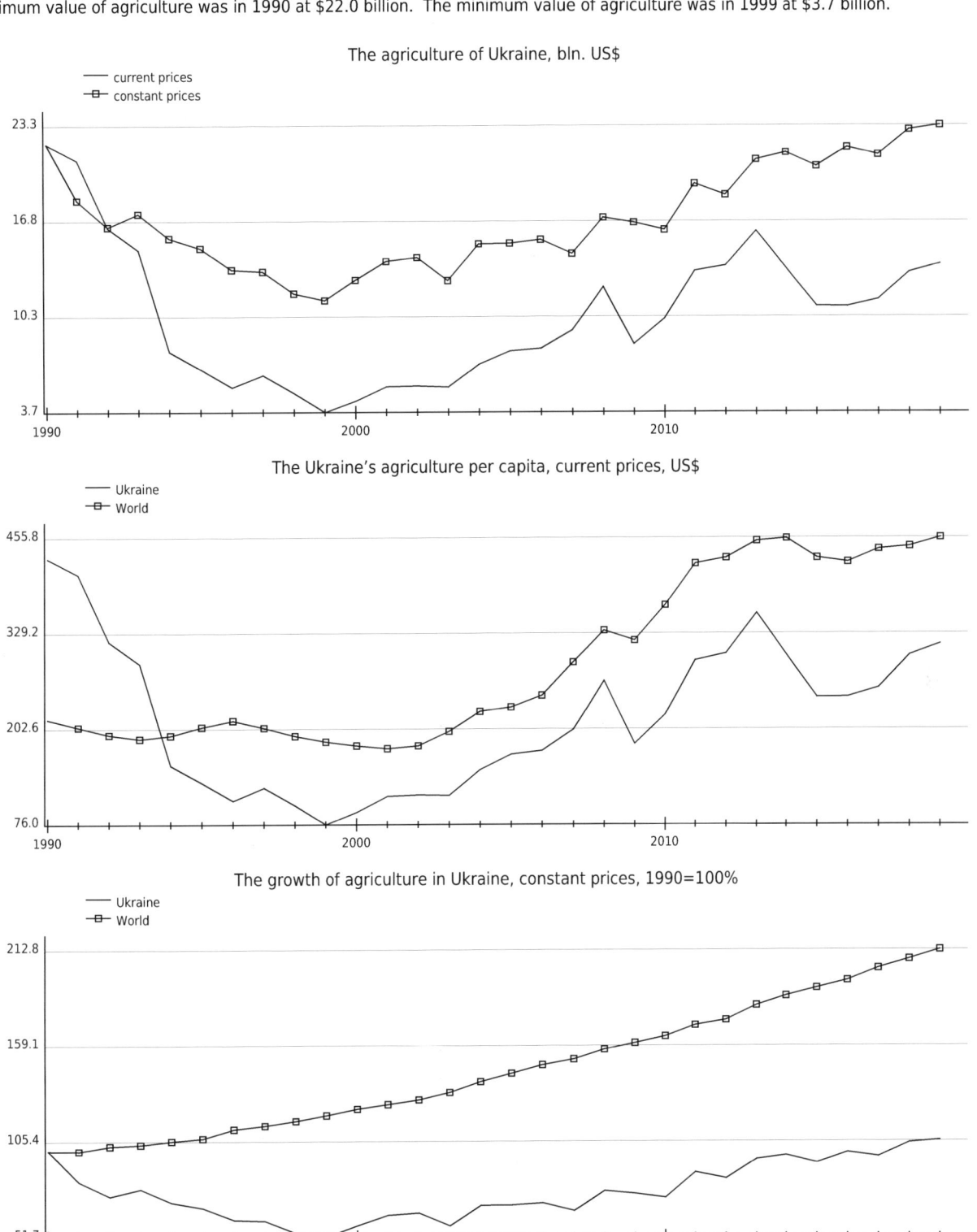

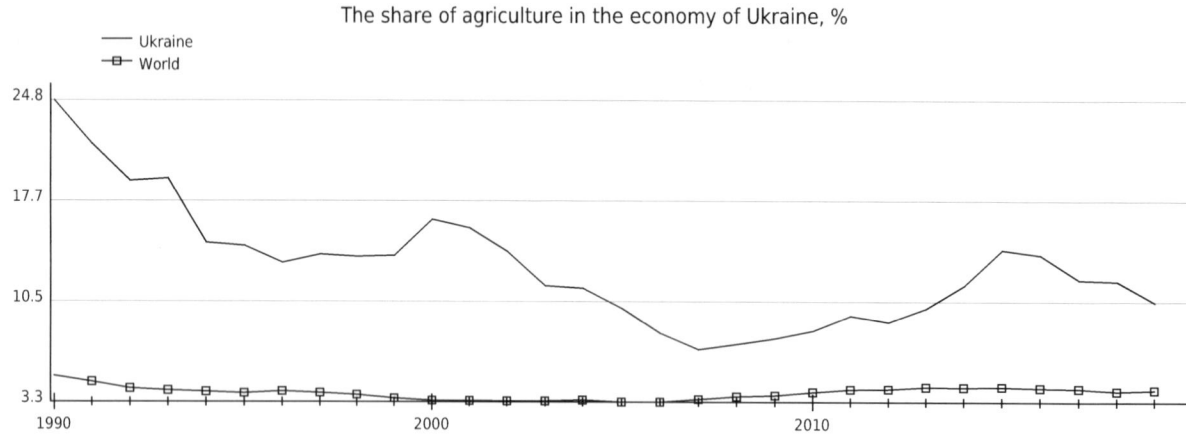

The 1990s

The sector of agriculture in Ukraine was $10.9 billion per year in the 1990s, ranked 25th in the world. The share in the world was 0.96%, and 3.9% in Europe.

The share of agriculture in the economy of Ukraine was 18.3% in the 1990s, ranked 72nd in the world, and was on a par with Serbia (18.3%), Zambia (18.2%), Romania (18.4%).

The agriculture per capita in Ukraine was $215.3 in the 1990s, ranked 94th in the world, and was on a par with Morocco ($215.1), Côte d'Ivoire ($214.7), Saint Kitts and Nevis ($217.3). The Ukrainian agriculture per capita was greater than agriculture per capita in the world ($199.8) by 7.8%, and was less than agriculture per capita in Europe ($382.2) by 43.7%.

The growth of agriculture in Ukraine was -7.1% in the 1990s, ranked 195th in the world, and was on a par with Kosovo (-7.1%). The growth of agriculture in Ukraine (-7.1%) was less than growth of agriculture in the world (2.2%), was less than growth of agriculture in Europe (-1.6%).

Comparison with neighbors. The agriculture of Ukraine was greater than in Poland ($6.2 billion), in Romania ($5.8 billion), in Hungary ($3.1 billion), in Belarus ($2.7 billion), in Bulgaria ($1.8 billion), and in Moldova ($743.1 million); but less than in Russia ($36.1 billion). The value added of agriculture per capita in Ukraine was greater than in Bulgaria ($208.4), in Moldova ($171.7), and in Poland ($162.3); but less than in Hungary ($300.6), in Belarus ($266.6), in Romania ($253.0), and in Russia ($243.9). The growth of agriculture in Ukraine was greater than in Moldova (-10.9%); but less than in Romania (1.2%), in Poland (-1.9%), in Bulgaria (-2.1%), in Hungary (-3.0%), in Belarus (-4.6%), and in Russia (-5.3%).

Comparison with leaders. The value of agriculture in Ukraine was less than in China ($139.0 billion), in the United States ($96.1 billion), in India ($91.4 billion), in Japan ($78.9 billion), and in Brazil ($36.8 billion). The value of agriculture per capita in Ukraine was greater than in China ($112.7) and in India ($95.6); but less than in Japan ($625.5), in the USA ($363.4), and in Brazil ($228.7). The growth of agriculture in Ukraine was less than in China (4.3%), in Brazil (3.0%), in India (2.8%), in the USA (2.6%), and in Japan (-1.8%).

The 2000s

The agriculture of Ukraine was $7.4 billion per year in the 2000s, ranked 39th in the world, and was on a par with Myanmar ($7.4 billion), Venezuela ($7.4 billion). The share in the world was 0.47%, and 2.6% in Europe.

The share of agriculture in the economy of Ukraine was 9.4% in the 2000s, ranked 99th in the world, and was on a par with Thailand (9.4%), Bosnia and Herzegovina (9.4%).

The Ukrainian agriculture per capita was $157.0 in the 2000s, ranked 141st in the world, and was on a par with Cambodia ($156.9), El Salvador ($156.3), Liechtenstein ($158.0). The Ukraine's agriculture per capita was less than agriculture per capita in the world ($240.3) by 34.7%, and was less than agriculture per capita in Europe ($387.0) in 2.5 times.

The growth of agriculture in Ukraine was 3.9% in the 2000s, ranked 46th in the world, and was on a par with Belize (3.9%), Niger (3.9%), Bangladesh (3.9%). The growth of agriculture in Ukraine (3.9%) was greater than growth of agriculture in the world (3.0%), was greater than growth of agriculture in Europe (1.2%).

Chapter IV. Agriculture

Comparison with neighbors. The agriculture of Ukraine was greater than in Hungary ($3.8 billion), in Belarus ($2.7 billion), in Bulgaria ($2.0 billion), and in Moldova ($472.5 million); but less than in Russia ($33.6 billion), in Poland ($8.7 billion), and in Romania ($8.3 billion). The sector of agriculture per capita in Ukraine was greater than in Moldova ($113.7); but less than in Romania ($385.4), in Hungary ($380.1), in Belarus ($276.1), in Bulgaria ($264.4), in Russia ($232.9), and in Poland ($227.7). The growth of agriculture in Ukraine was greater than in Russia (3.6%), in Poland (2.8%), in Hungary (2.5%), in Moldova (0.095%), in Romania (-0.50%), and in Bulgaria (-2.7%); but less than in Belarus (5.4%).

Comparison with leaders. The sector of agriculture in Ukraine was less than in China ($297.7 billion), in India ($147.6 billion), in the United States ($122.5 billion), in Japan ($57.1 billion), and in Nigeria ($47.6 billion). The Ukrainian agriculture per capita was greater than in India ($129.7); but less than in Japan ($445.6), in the USA ($416.9), in Nigeria ($346.4), and in China ($224.5). The growth of agriculture in Ukraine was greater than in the United States (3.6%), in India (2.0%), and in Japan (-1.3%); but less than in Nigeria (10.1%) and in China (4.0%).

The 2010s

The agriculture of Ukraine was $12.7 billion per year in the 2010s, ranked 42nd in the world, and was on a par with Tanzania ($12.9 billion). The share in the world was 0.40%, and 3.5% in Europe.

The share of agriculture in the economy of Ukraine was 10.8% in the 2010s, ranked 78th in the world, and was on a par with Algeria (10.8%), Macedonia (10.7%).

The Ukrainian agriculture per capita was $283.3 in the 2010s, ranked 136th in the world, and was on a par with Luxembourg ($283.2), Southern Asia ($280.8), Cuba ($286.0). The value added of agriculture per capita in Ukraine was less than agriculture per capita in the world ($432.1) by 34.4%, and was less than agriculture per capita in Europe ($491.7) by 42.4%.

The growth of agriculture in Ukraine was 3.4% in the 2010s, ranked 57th in the world, and was on a par with Zimbabwe (3.4%), Malawi (3.4%), DR Congo (3.4%). The growth of agriculture in Ukraine (3.4%) was greater than growth of agriculture in the world (2.9%), was greater than growth of agriculture in Europe (0.73%).

Comparison with neighbors. The Ukrainian agriculture was 37.7% higher than in Romania ($9.2 billion), 2.5 times higher than in Hungary ($5.2 billion), 2.8 times higher than in Belarus ($4.5 billion), 5.5 times higher than in Bulgaria ($2.3 billion), and 12.5 times higher than in Moldova ($1.0 billion); but 4.7 times lower than in Russia ($60.3 billion) and 10.5% lower than in Poland ($14.2 billion). The Ukrainian agriculture per capita was 13.2% higher than in Moldova ($250.3); but 46.3% lower than in Hungary ($527.7), 41.2% lower than in Belarus ($482.1), 38.9% lower than in Romania ($463.7), 32.0% lower than in Russia ($416.5), 24.2% lower than in Poland ($373.5), and 11.5% lower than in Bulgaria ($320.2). The growth of agriculture in Ukraine was greater than in Romania (2.3%), in Belarus (1.9%), in Russia (1.2%), in Hungary (0.14%), in Bulgaria (0.069%), and in Poland (-1.6%); but less than in Moldova (11.2%).

Comparison with leaders. The sector of agriculture in Ukraine was 69.6 times lower than in China ($886.2 billion), 28.5 times lower than in India ($363.4 billion), 14.2 times lower than in the United States ($180.3 billion), 9.7 times lower than in Indonesia ($124.1 billion), and 7.5 times lower than in Nigeria ($95.8 billion). The value added of agriculture per capita in Ukraine was 1.5% higher than in India ($279.1); but 2.2 times lower than in China ($631.9), 49.8% lower than in the United States ($564.3), 47.0% lower than in Nigeria ($534.6), and 41.4% lower than in Indonesia ($483.6). The growth of agriculture in Ukraine was greater than in the United States (2.0%); but less than in India (4.1%), in Indonesia (3.9%), in China (3.8%), and in Nigeria (3.6%).

Chapter V. Industry

Mining, Manufacturing, Utilities (ISIC C-E)

The sector of industry in Ukraine grew up from $21.5 billion per year in the 1990s to $28.9 billion per year in the 2010s, that is by $7.4 billion or 34.5%. The change occurred at $6.6 billion due to a 1.3-fold increase in prices, as also at $3.3 billion due to a 1.2-fold increase in productivity, as well as at -$2.5 billion due to the drop in population. The average annual growth in industry is -2.3%. The minimum value of industry was in 2000 at $9.1 billion. The maximum value of industry was in 2008 at $46.5 billion.

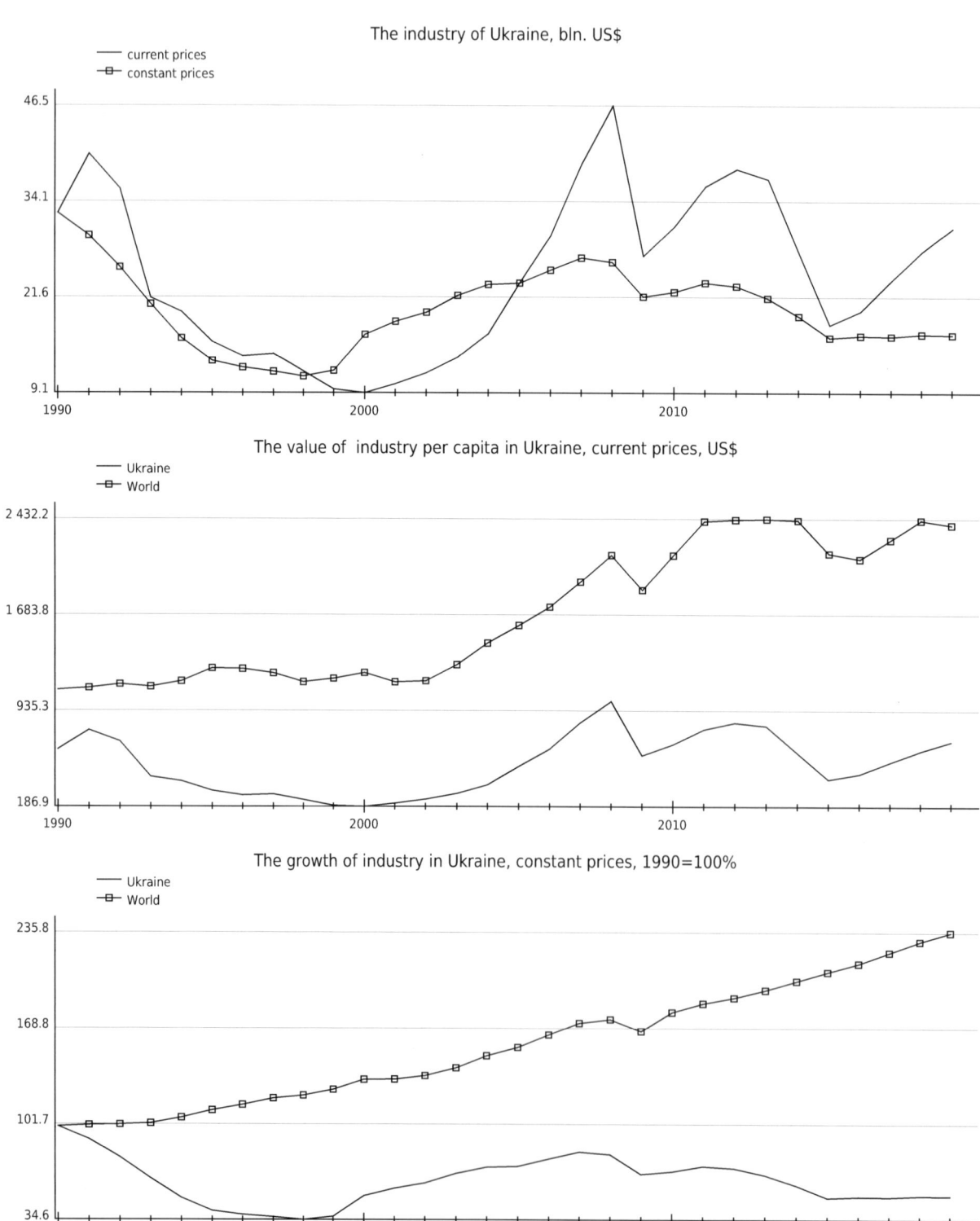

Chapter V. Industry

The share of industry in the economy of Ukraine, %

The 1990s

The value added of industry in Ukraine was $21.5 billion per year in the 1990s, ranked 35th in the world, and was on a par with Colombia ($21.0 billion). The share in the world was 0.32%, and 1.00% in Europe.

The share of industry in the economy of Ukraine was 35.9% in the 1990s, ranked 20th in the world, and was on a par with San Marino (35.9%), Malaysia (36.1%), Belarus (35.7%).

The industry per capita in Ukraine was $423.4 in the 1990s, ranked 102nd in the world, and was on a par with Angola ($430.7), Peru ($433.7). The value of industry per capita in Ukraine was less than industry per capita in the world ($1 175.6) in 2.8 times, and was less than industry per capita in Europe ($2 961.4) in 7.0 times.

The growth of industry in Ukraine was -10.5% in the 1990s, ranked 199th in the world. The growth of industry in Ukraine (-10.5%) was less than growth of industry in the world (2.5%), was less than growth of industry in Europe (0.0047%).

Comparison with neighbors. The industry of Ukraine was greater than in Romania ($10.6 billion), in Hungary ($9.8 billion), in Belarus ($5.3 billion), in Bulgaria ($2.8 billion), and in Moldova ($689.9 million); but less than in Russia ($138.6 billion) and in Poland ($33.8 billion). The industry per capita in Ukraine was greater than in Bulgaria ($329.9) and in Moldova ($159.4); but less than in Hungary ($951.3), in Russia ($937.0), in Poland ($880.1), in Belarus ($528.4), and in Romania ($459.2). The growth of industry in Ukraine was greater than in Moldova (-13.0%); but less than in Poland (1.9%), in Hungary (1.0%), in Belarus (-1.4%), in Romania (-4.6%), in Bulgaria (-5.2%), and in Russia (-6.8%).

Comparison with leaders. The value added of industry in Ukraine was less than in the USA ($1.5 trillion), in Japan ($1.2 trillion), in Germany ($534.0 billion), in China ($285.9 billion), and in the United Kingdom ($268.6 billion). The value added of industry per capita in Ukraine was greater than in China ($231.9); but less than in Japan ($9.4 thousand), in Germany ($6.6 thousand), in the USA ($5.7 thousand), and in the UK ($4.6 thousand). The growth of industry in Ukraine was less than in China (13.1%), in the USA (2.8%), in Japan (1.3%), in the UK (1.2%), and in Germany (0.33%).

The 2000s

The value added of industry in Ukraine was $22.7 billion per year in the 2000s, ranked 53rd in the world, and was on a par with Peru ($22.7 billion), Hungary ($22.3 billion). The share in the world was 0.22%, and 0.78% in Europe.

The share of industry in the economy of Ukraine was 28.8% in the 2000s, ranked 48th in the world, and was on a par with Central Asia (28.8%), Eastern Europe (28.5%).

The value added of industry per capita in Ukraine was $481.3 in the 2000s, ranked 122nd in the world, and was on a par with Syria ($480.5), Central Asia ($482.9), Grenada ($488.4). The value of industry per capita in Ukraine was less than industry per capita in the world ($1 573.8) in 3.3 times, and was less than industry per capita in Europe ($4 000.9) in 8.3 times.

The growth of industry in Ukraine was 6.1% in the 2000s, ranked 35th in the world. The growth of industry in Ukraine (6.1%) was greater than growth of industry in the world (2.9%), was greater than growth of industry in Europe (0.63%).

Comparison with neighbors. The Ukrainian industry was greater than in Hungary ($22.3 billion), in Belarus ($9.1 billion), in Bulgaria ($5.8 billion), and in Moldova ($571.8 million); but less than in Russia ($207.1 billion), in Poland ($66.8 billion), and in Romania

($26.4 billion). The Ukraine's industry per capita was greater than in Moldova ($137.6); but less than in Hungary ($2.2 thousand), in Poland ($1 738.2), in Russia ($1 435.1), in Romania ($1 232.8), in Belarus ($942.2), and in Bulgaria ($745.0). The growth of industry in Ukraine was greater than in Romania (5.3%), in Bulgaria (5.0%), in Poland (4.2%), in Russia (3.5%), in Hungary (1.5%), and in Moldova (1.4%); but less than in Belarus (7.8%).

Comparison with leaders. The sector of industry in Ukraine was less than in the USA ($2.1 trillion), in Japan ($1.1 trillion), in China ($1.1 trillion), in Germany ($629.4 billion), and in the United Kingdom ($345.1 billion). The value of industry per capita in Ukraine was less than in Japan ($8.8 thousand), in Germany ($7.7 thousand), in the United States ($7.1 thousand), in the UK ($5.7 thousand), and in China ($795.3). The growth of industry in Ukraine was greater than in the USA (1.5%), in Germany (0.19%), in Japan (0.15%), and in the UK (-1.1%); but less than in China (11.1%).

The 2010s

The value added of industry in Ukraine was $28.9 billion per year in the 2010s, ranked 59th in the world. The share in the world was 0.17%, and 0.76% in Europe.

The share of industry in the economy of Ukraine was 24.4% in the 2010s, ranked 73rd in the world, and was on a par with the Philippines (24.2%).

The sector of industry per capita in Ukraine was $642.8 in the 2010s, ranked 132nd in the world, and was on a par with Saint Lucia ($641.2), Morocco ($632.6), Armenia ($653.5). The value of industry per capita in Ukraine was less than industry per capita in the world ($2 320.9) in 3.6 times, and was less than industry per capita in Europe ($5 088.1) in 7.9 times.

The growth of industry in Ukraine was -2.6% in the 2010s, ranked 200th in the world. The growth of industry in Ukraine (-2.6%) was less than growth of industry in the world (3.5%), was less than growth of industry in Europe (2.0%).

Comparison with neighbors. The sector of industry in Ukraine was 76.6% higher than in Belarus ($16.4 billion), 2.6 times higher than in Bulgaria ($11.0 billion), and 21.3 times higher than in Moldova ($1.4 billion); but 14.2 times lower than in Russia ($410.4 billion), 4.0 times lower than in Poland ($116.0 billion), 42.0% lower than in Romania ($49.8 billion), and 4.7% lower than in Hungary ($30.3 billion). The industry per capita in Ukraine was 92.9% higher than in Moldova ($333.3); but 4.8 times lower than in Hungary ($3.1 thousand), 4.7 times lower than in Poland ($3.0 thousand), 4.4 times lower than in Russia ($2.8 thousand), 3.9 times lower than in Romania ($2.5 thousand), 2.7 times lower than in Belarus ($1 734.9), and 2.4 times lower than in Bulgaria ($1 530.9). The growth of industry in Ukraine was less than in Hungary (5.8%), in Moldova (5.6%), in Poland (4.5%), in Belarus (2.5%), in Bulgaria (2.5%), in Romania (2.1%), and in Russia (1.7%).

Comparison with leaders. The value of industry in Ukraine was 127.4 times lower than in China ($3.7 trillion), 94.9 times lower than in the USA ($2.7 trillion), 41.2 times lower than in Japan ($1.2 trillion), 29.1 times lower than in Germany ($840.0 billion), and 15.3 times lower than in India ($443.4 billion). The Ukraine's industry per capita was 88.7% higher than in India ($340.6); but 16.0 times lower than in Germany ($10.3 thousand), 14.5 times lower than in Japan ($9.3 thousand), 13.4 times lower than in the United States ($8.6 thousand), and 4.1 times lower than in China ($2.6 thousand). The growth of industry in Ukraine was less than in China (7.5%), in India (6.5%), in Germany (3.2%), in Japan (2.6%), and in the United States (2.2%).

Chapter 5.1. Manufacturing

(ISIC D)

The manufacturing of Ukraine abated from $20.4 billion per year in the 1990s to $16.4 billion per year in the 2010s, that is by -$4.0 billion or 19.8%. The change occurred at -$428.4 million due to a 1.0-fold decrease in prices, as also at -$1.3 billion due to a 1.1-fold decrease in productivity, as well as at -$2.3 billion due to the decline in population. The average annual growth in manufacturing is -3.1%. The maximum value of manufacturing was in 1991 at $38.8 billion. The minimum value of manufacturing was in 2000 at $5.6 billion.

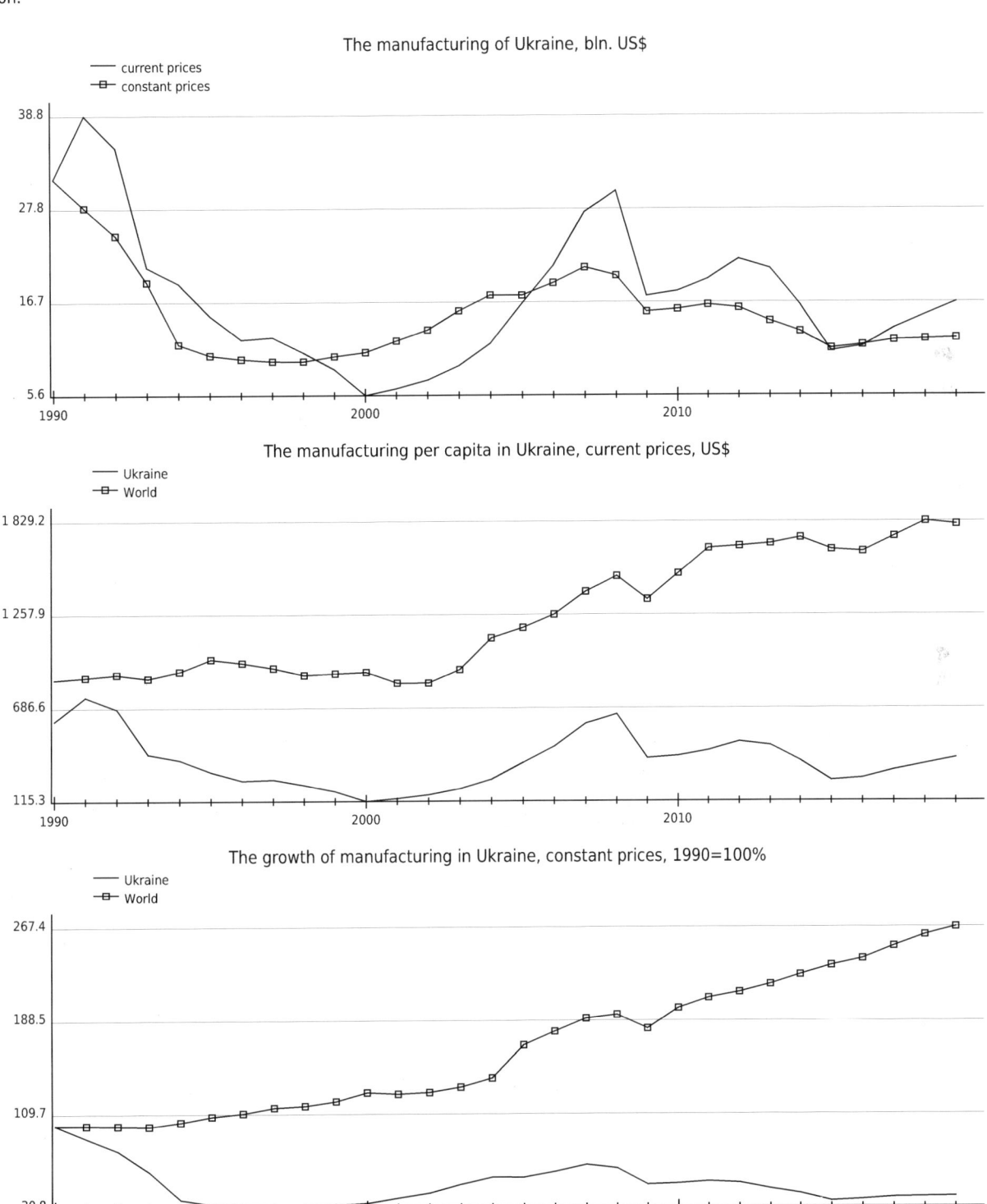

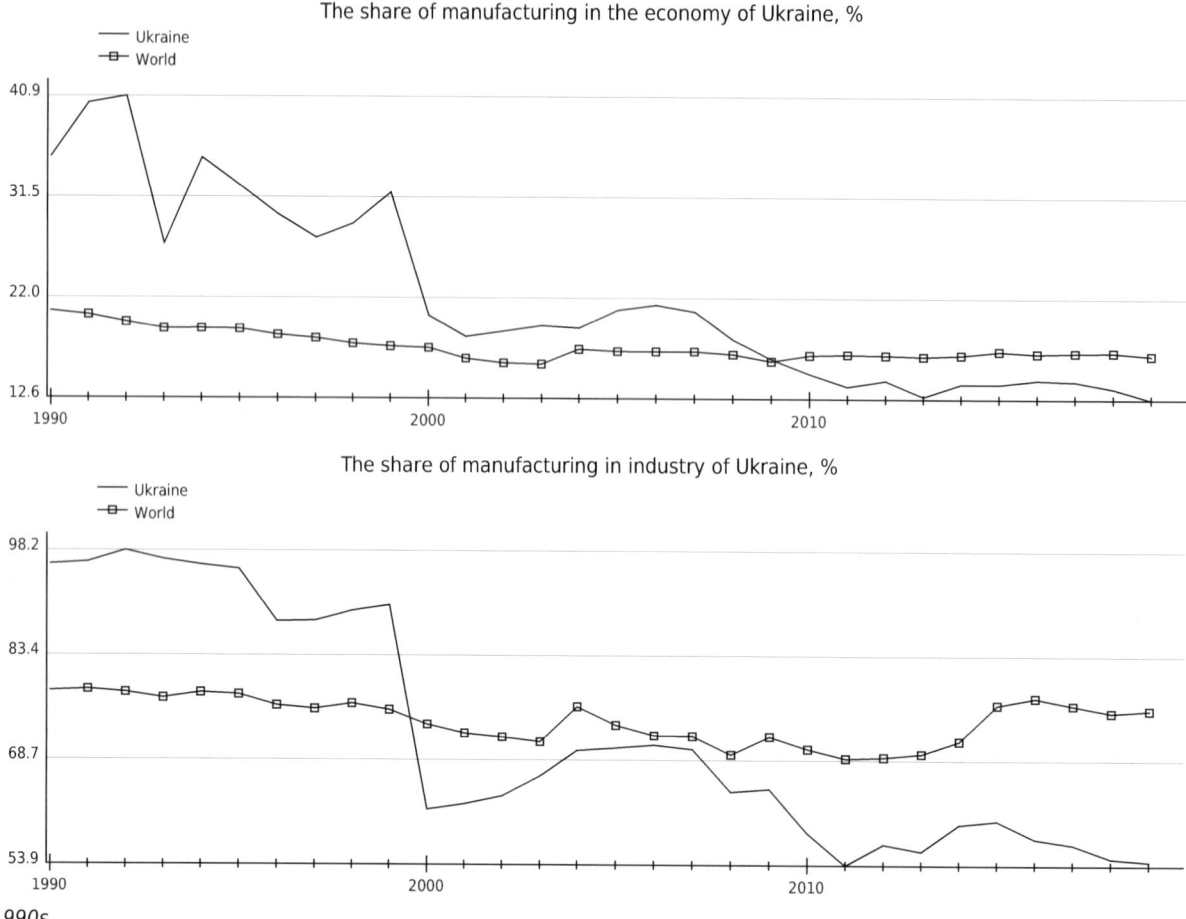

The 1990s

The value added of manufacturing in Ukraine was $20.4 billion per year in the 1990s, ranked 28th in the world, and was on a par with Malaysia ($20.1 billion). The share in the world was 0.39%, and 1.1% in Europe.

The share of manufacturing in the economy of Ukraine was 34.1% in the 1990s, ranked 5th in the world.

The value of manufacturing per capita in Ukraine was $402.2 in the 1990s, ranked 84th in the world, and was on a par with Colombia ($408.1). The value added of manufacturing per capita in Ukraine was less than manufacturing per capita in the world ($908.4) in 2.3 times, and was less than manufacturing per capita in Europe ($2 443.3) in 6.1 times.

The growth of manufacturing in Ukraine was -11.7% in the 1990s, ranked 200th in the world. The growth of manufacturing in Ukraine (-11.7%) was less than growth of manufacturing in the world (2.0%), was less than growth of manufacturing in Europe (0.24%).

Comparison with neighbors. The manufacturing of Ukraine was greater than in Romania ($8.5 billion), in Hungary ($8.0 billion), in Belarus ($5.0 billion), in Bulgaria ($1.9 billion), and in Moldova ($595.1 million); but less than in Russia ($92.7 billion) and in Poland ($25.3 billion). The value of manufacturing per capita in Ukraine was greater than in Romania ($371.3), in Bulgaria ($220.2), and in Moldova ($137.5); but less than in Hungary ($772.2), in Poland ($659.9), in Russia ($626.6), and in Belarus ($491.9). The growth of manufacturing in Ukraine was greater than in Moldova (-13.6%); but less than in Poland (3.6%), in Hungary (2.5%), in Belarus (-0.89%), in Romania (-4.9%), in Bulgaria (-5.4%), and in Russia (-6.8%).

Comparison with leaders. The Ukraine's manufacturing was less than in the United States ($1.2 trillion), in Japan ($1.0 trillion), in Germany ($468.8 billion), in Italy ($227.8 billion), and in France ($215.0 billion). The manufacturing per capita in Ukraine was less than in Japan ($8.3 thousand), in Germany ($5.8 thousand), in the USA ($4.7 thousand), in Italy ($4.0 thousand), and in France ($3.6 thousand). The growth of manufacturing in Ukraine was less than in the USA (3.2%), in France (2.4%), in Italy (1.2%), in Japan (1.1%), and in Germany (0.26%).

The 2000s

The value of manufacturing in Ukraine was $15.3 billion per year in the 2000s, ranked 49th in the world, and was on a par with Central

Chapter 5.1. Manufacturing

Asia ($15.3 billion). The share in the world was 0.21%, and 0.66% in Europe.

The share of manufacturing in the economy of Ukraine was 19.3% in the 2000s, ranked 38th in the world, and was on a par with Trinidad and Tobago (19.3%), Eastern Europe (19.3%), Sweden (19.3%).

The sector of manufacturing per capita in Ukraine was $323.2 in the 2000s, ranked 109th in the world, and was on a par with Jamaica ($328.3). The Ukraine's manufacturing per capita was less than manufacturing per capita in the world ($1 138.1) in 3.5 times, and was less than manufacturing per capita in Europe ($3 162.1) in 9.8 times.

The growth of manufacturing in Ukraine was 4.3% in the 2000s, ranked 74th in the world, and was on a par with Western Asia (4.2%), Antigua and Barbuda (4.3%). The growth of manufacturing in Ukraine (4.3%) was greater than growth of manufacturing in the world (4.2%), was greater than growth of manufacturing in Europe (0.69%).

Comparison with neighbors. The value of manufacturing in Ukraine was greater than in Belarus ($7.3 billion), in Bulgaria ($4.0 billion), and in Moldova ($453.5 million); but less than in Russia ($120.8 billion), in Poland ($49.3 billion), in Romania ($22.1 billion), and in Hungary ($19.0 billion). The Ukraine's manufacturing per capita was greater than in Moldova ($109.1); but less than in Hungary ($1 880.6), in Poland ($1 281.9), in Romania ($1 032.6), in Russia ($837.1), in Belarus ($754.9), and in Bulgaria ($520.2). The growth of manufacturing in Ukraine was greater than in Russia (3.6%), in Hungary (2.5%), and in Moldova (2.1%); but less than in Belarus (10.0%), in Poland (7.0%), in Bulgaria (6.6%), and in Romania (6.0%).

Comparison with leaders. The value of manufacturing in Ukraine was less than in the United States ($1.6 trillion), in China ($1.1 trillion), in Japan ($992.9 billion), in Germany ($551.4 billion), and in Italy ($277.2 billion). The value added of manufacturing per capita in Ukraine was less than in Japan ($7.7 thousand), in Germany ($6.8 thousand), in the United States ($5.6 thousand), in Italy ($4.8 thousand), and in China ($815.3). The growth of manufacturing in Ukraine was greater than in the USA (1.6%), in Japan (0.32%), in Germany (0.097%), and in Italy (-1.3%).

The 2010s

The value of manufacturing in Ukraine was $16.4 billion per year in the 2010s, ranked 58th in the world, and was on a par with Qatar ($16.3 billion), Morocco ($16.6 billion). The share in the world was 0.13%, and 0.56% in Europe.

The share of manufacturing in the economy of Ukraine was 13.8% in the 2010s, ranked 77th in the world, and was on a par with Bosnia and Herzegovina (13.9%).

The manufacturing per capita in Ukraine was $364.1 in the 2010s, ranked 120th in the world, and was on a par with Northern Africa ($367.7), Georgia ($359.4), Antigua and Barbuda ($357.3). The Ukrainian manufacturing per capita was less than manufacturing per capita in the world ($1 697.4) in 4.7 times, and was less than manufacturing per capita in Europe ($3 895.6) in 10.7 times.

The growth of manufacturing in Ukraine was -2.2% in the 2010s, ranked 194th in the world. The growth of manufacturing in Ukraine (-2.2%) was less than growth of manufacturing in the world (3.9%), was less than growth of manufacturing in Europe (2.5%).

Comparison with neighbors. The value of manufacturing in Ukraine was 18.6% higher than in Belarus ($13.8 billion), 2.2 times higher than in Bulgaria ($7.5 billion), and 15.9 times higher than in Moldova ($1.0 billion); but 13.0 times lower than in Russia ($212.1 billion), 5.3 times lower than in Poland ($86.2 billion), 2.5 times lower than in Romania ($40.4 billion), and 37.8% lower than in Hungary ($26.3 billion). The Ukraine's manufacturing per capita was 44.2% higher than in Moldova ($252.4); but 7.4 times lower than in Hungary ($2.7 thousand), 6.2 times lower than in Poland ($2.3 thousand), 5.6 times lower than in Romania ($2.0 thousand), 4.0 times lower than in Russia ($1 465.5), 4.0 times lower than in Belarus ($1 463.0), and 2.9 times lower than in Bulgaria ($1 039.4). The growth of manufacturing in Ukraine was less than in Moldova (7.0%), in Poland (5.4%), in Bulgaria (3.1%), in Hungary (3.1%), in Belarus (2.7%), in Romania (2.5%), and in Russia (2.1%).

Comparison with leaders. The sector of manufacturing in Ukraine was 190.3 times lower than in China ($3.1 trillion), 126.5 times lower than in the USA ($2.1 trillion), 64.8 times lower than in Japan ($1.1 trillion), 44.9 times lower than in Germany ($735.2 billion), and 23.9 times lower than in South Korea ($390.5 billion). The Ukraine's manufacturing per capita was 24.7 times lower than in Germany ($9.0 thousand), 22.8 times lower than in Japan ($8.3 thousand), 21.2 times lower than in South Korea ($7.7 thousand), 17.8 times lower than in the USA ($6.5 thousand), and 6.1 times lower than in China ($2.2 thousand). The growth of manufacturing in Ukraine was less than in China (7.5%), in South Korea (3.8%), in Germany (3.5%), in Japan (3.0%), and in the United States (1.9%).

Chapter VI. Construction

(ISIC F)

The value added of construction in Ukraine lessened from $4.5 billion per year in the 1990s to $3.5 billion per year in the 2010s, that is by -$940.4 million or 21.1%. The change occurred at $2.8 billion due to a 4.7-fold increase in prices, as also at -$3.2 billion due to a 5.3-fold decrease in productivity, as well as at -$509.5 million due to the downfall in population. The average annual growth in construction is -8.3%. The maximum value of construction was in 1991 at $8.1 billion. The minimum value of construction was in 2000 at $1.1 billion.

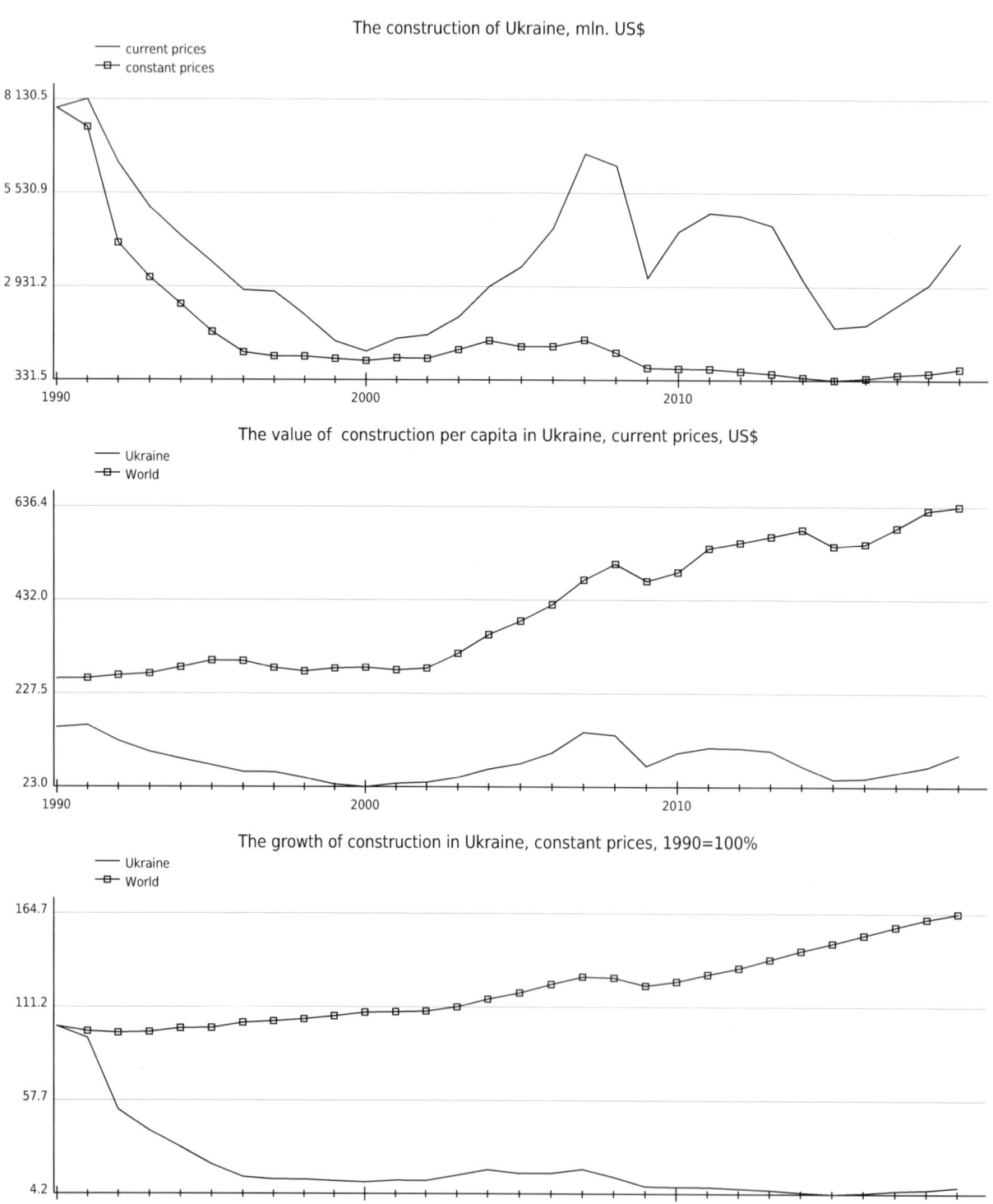

Chapter VI. Construction

The 1990s

The value added of construction in Ukraine was $4.5 billion per year in the 1990s, ranked 41st in the world, and was on a par with Algeria ($4.6 billion). The share in the world was 0.28%, and 0.81% in Europe.

The share of construction in the economy of Ukraine was 7.5% in the 1990s, ranked 41st in the world, and was on a par with Uzbekistan (7.4%), the TCI (7.4%), Tonga (7.5%).

The value of construction per capita in Ukraine was $87.9 in the 1990s, ranked 114th in the world, and was on a par with Eswatini ($86.3), Paraguay ($90.0). The construction per capita in Ukraine was less than construction per capita in the world ($278.6) in 3.2 times, and was less than construction per capita in Europe ($760.7) in 8.7 times.

The growth of construction in Ukraine was -21.3% in the 1990s, ranked 205th in the world. The growth of construction in Ukraine (-21.3%) was less than growth of construction in the world (0.71%), was less than growth of construction in Europe (-1.7%).

Comparison with neighbors. The sector of construction in Ukraine was greater than in Hungary ($2.0 billion), in Romania ($1.9 billion), in Belarus ($1.0 billion), in Bulgaria ($562.9 million), and in Moldova ($236.9 million); but less than in Russia ($34.1 billion) and in Poland ($10.3 billion). The value added of construction per capita in Ukraine was greater than in Romania ($81.2), in Bulgaria ($66.7), and in Moldova ($54.7); but less than in Poland ($269.0), in Russia ($230.4), in Hungary ($189.1), and in Belarus ($102.1). The growth of construction in Ukraine was greater than in Moldova (-21.8%); but less than in Poland (4.8%), in Romania (0.74%), in Bulgaria (-1.5%), in Hungary (-2.1%), in Belarus (-8.5%), and in Russia (-12.1%).

Comparison with leaders. The sector of construction in Ukraine was less than in Japan ($343.2 billion), in the USA ($299.1 billion), in Germany ($125.2 billion), in the United Kingdom ($69.8 billion), and in France ($68.8 billion). The value added of construction per capita in Ukraine was less than in Japan ($2.7 thousand), in Germany ($1 552.3), in the UK ($1 205.1), in France ($1 158.8), and in the USA ($1 131.2). The growth of construction in Ukraine was less than in the USA (1.8%), in Germany (-0.047%), in the UK (-0.34%), in France (-0.65%), and in Japan (-1.0%).

The 2000s

The value added of construction in Ukraine was $3.3 billion per year in the 2000s, ranked 56th in the world. The share in the world was 0.13%, and 0.40% in Europe.

The share of construction in the economy of Ukraine was 4.2% in the 2000s, ranked 162nd in the world, and was on a par with Nauru (4.2%), Somalia (4.2%), Oman (4.2%).

The construction per capita in Ukraine was $70.6 in the 2000s, ranked 148th in the world, and was on a par with the Philippines ($69.6), the Federated States of Micronesia ($71.8), Moldova ($69.3). The sector of construction per capita in Ukraine was less than construction per capita in the world ($381.3) in 5.4 times, and was less than construction per capita in Europe ($1 147.4) in 16.3 times.

The growth of construction in Ukraine was -3.1% in the 2000s, ranked 204th in the world. The growth of construction in Ukraine (-3.1%) was less than growth of construction in the world (1.5%), was less than growth of construction in Europe (0.97%).

Comparison with neighbors. The value of construction in Ukraine was greater than in Belarus ($2.3 billion), in Bulgaria ($1.9 billion), and in Moldova ($288.1 million); but less than in Russia ($40.5 billion), in Poland ($21.3 billion), in Romania ($9.2 billion), and in

Hungary ($4.6 billion). The construction per capita in Ukraine was greater than in Moldova ($69.3); but less than in Poland ($553.8), in Hungary ($451.6), in Romania ($428.2), in Russia ($280.3), in Bulgaria ($246.1), and in Belarus ($240.2). The growth of construction in Ukraine was less than in Belarus (12.5%), in Romania (11.7%), in Russia (8.1%), in Bulgaria (7.5%), in Moldova (3.9%), in Hungary (1.4%), and in Poland (1.0%).

Comparison with leaders. The value of construction in Ukraine was less than in the USA ($583.0 billion), in Japan ($270.5 billion), in China ($150.1 billion), in the United Kingdom ($132.1 billion), and in Spain ($111.8 billion). The construction per capita in Ukraine was less than in Spain ($2.6 thousand), in the United Kingdom ($2.2 thousand), in Japan ($2.1 thousand), in the United States ($1 983.7), and in China ($113.1). The growth of construction in Ukraine was greater than in Japan (-3.9%); but less than in China (11.9%), in Spain (1.7%), in the UK (0.17%), and in the USA (-2.6%).

The 2010s

The construction of Ukraine was $3.5 billion per year in the 2010s, ranked 75th in the world. The share in the world was 0.084%, and 0.33% in Europe.

The share of construction in the economy of Ukraine was 3.0% in the 2010s, ranked 192nd in the world, and was on a par with Fiji (3.0%).

The construction per capita in Ukraine was $78.3 in the 2010s, ranked 173rd in the world. The value of construction per capita in Ukraine was less than construction per capita in the world ($572.1) in 7.3 times, and was less than construction per capita in Europe ($1 415.6) in 18.1 times.

The growth of construction in Ukraine was -0.4% in the 2010s, ranked 169th in the world. The growth of construction in Ukraine (-0.40%) was less than growth of construction in the world (2.9%), was less than growth of construction in Europe (0.50%).

Comparison with neighbors. The construction of Ukraine was 43.6% higher than in Bulgaria ($2.5 billion) and 5.3 times higher than in Moldova ($664.9 million); but 32.6 times lower than in Russia ($114.9 billion), 10.1 times lower than in Poland ($35.5 billion), 3.6 times lower than in Romania ($12.5 billion), 31.5% lower than in Hungary ($5.1 billion), and 24.6% lower than in Belarus ($4.7 billion). The value added of construction per capita in Ukraine was 11.9 times lower than in Poland ($932.6), 10.1 times lower than in Russia ($793.7), 8.0 times lower than in Romania ($627.1), 6.7 times lower than in Hungary ($524.2), 6.3 times lower than in Belarus ($495.0), 4.3 times lower than in Bulgaria ($339.6), and 2.1 times lower than in Moldova ($163.4). The growth of construction in Ukraine was greater than in Belarus (-0.98%), in Romania (-2.2%), and in Bulgaria (-2.6%); but less than in Moldova (6.8%), in Hungary (3.6%), in Poland (2.8%), and in Russia (1.8%).

Comparison with leaders. The Ukraine's construction was 207.6 times lower than in China ($731.1 billion), 193.4 times lower than in the USA ($680.8 billion), 79.1 times lower than in Japan ($278.7 billion), 47.7 times lower than in India ($168.1 billion), and 43.5 times lower than in Germany ($153.2 billion). The sector of construction per capita in Ukraine was 27.8 times lower than in Japan ($2.2 thousand), 27.2 times lower than in the USA ($2.1 thousand), 23.9 times lower than in Germany ($1 871.9), 6.7 times lower than in China ($521.3), and 39.3% lower than in India ($129.1). The growth of construction in Ukraine was less than in China (8.2%), in India (5.2%), in Germany (1.8%), in Japan (1.7%), and in the United States (1.4%).

Chapter VII. Transportation

Transport, storage and communication (ISIC I)

The value added of transportation in Ukraine enlarged from $6.1 billion per year in the 1990s to $14.4 billion per year in the 2010s, that is by $8.2 billion or 2.3 times. The change occurred at $8.7 billion due to a 2.5-fold increase in prices, as also at $242.9 million due to a 1.0-fold increase in productivity, as well as at -$701.6 million due to the falling in population. The average annual growth in transportation is -2.5%. The minimum value of transportation was in 2000 at $3.8 billion. The maximum value of transportation was in 2013 at $19.1 billion.

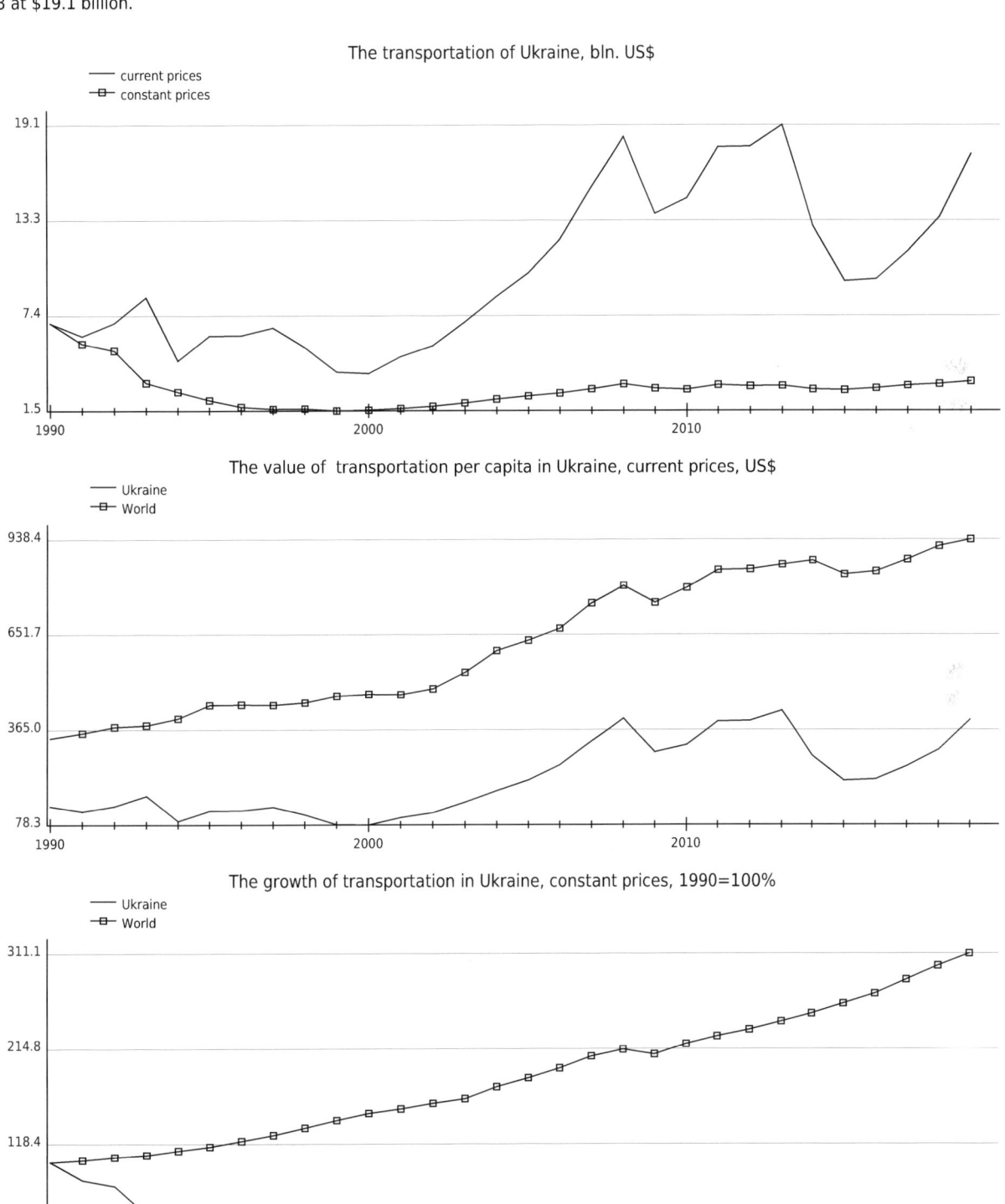

The 1990s

The Ukraine's transportation was $6.1 billion per year in the 1990s, ranked 40th in the world. The share in the world was 0.26%, and 0.78% in Europe.

The share of transportation in the economy of Ukraine was 10.3% in the 1990s, ranked 47th in the world, and was on a par with Hong Kong (10.3%), Finland (10.3%).

The Ukrainian transportation per capita was $121.0 in the 1990s, ranked 118th in the world, and was on a par with Romania ($120.2), Papua New Guinea ($119.2), Samoa ($118.2). The value added of transportation per capita in Ukraine was less than transportation per capita in the world ($409.5) in 3.4 times, and was less than transportation per capita in Europe ($1 080.1) in 8.9 times.

The growth of transportation in Ukraine was -15.5% in the 1990s, ranked 205th in the world. The growth of transportation in Ukraine (-15.5%) was less than growth of transportation in the world (4.0%), was less than growth of transportation in Europe (2.4%).

Comparison with neighbors. The value of transportation in Ukraine was greater than in Hungary ($3.6 billion), in Romania ($2.8 billion), in Belarus ($1.5 billion), in Bulgaria ($1.2 billion), and in Moldova ($122.3 million); but less than in Russia ($38.4 billion) and in Poland ($8.5 billion). The value of transportation per capita in Ukraine was greater than in Romania ($120.2) and in Moldova ($28.3); but less than in Hungary ($347.6), in Russia ($259.8), in Poland ($222.1), in Belarus ($150.4), and in Bulgaria ($136.4). The growth of transportation in Ukraine was greater than in Moldova (-17.9%); but less than in Poland (3.2%), in Bulgaria (2.4%), in Hungary (-1.5%), in Romania (-3.8%), in Belarus (-6.7%), and in Russia (-7.1%).

Comparison with leaders. The Ukrainian transportation was less than in the United States ($702.6 billion), in Japan ($373.9 billion), in Germany ($144.3 billion), in France ($118.7 billion), and in the United Kingdom ($117.6 billion). The sector of transportation per capita in Ukraine was less than in Japan ($3.0 thousand), in the USA ($2.7 thousand), in the UK ($2.0 thousand), in France ($1 999.2), and in Germany ($1 789.0). The growth of transportation in Ukraine was less than in the United States (5.0%), in France (4.8%), in the United Kingdom (4.7%), in Germany (3.9%), and in Japan (3.0%).

The 2000s

The value of transportation in Ukraine was $9.9 billion per year in the 2000s, ranked 47th in the world, and was on a par with Eastern Africa ($9.9 billion), Malaysia ($9.8 billion). The share in the world was 0.25%, and 0.73% in Europe.

The share of transportation in the economy of Ukraine was 12.6% in the 2000s, ranked 26th in the world, and was on a par with Tunisia (12.6%).

The sector of transportation per capita in Ukraine was $210.2 in the 2000s, ranked 122nd in the world, and was on a par with Micronesia ($209.0), El Salvador ($213.7). The Ukrainian transportation per capita was less than transportation per capita in the world ($621.1) in 3.0 times, and was less than transportation per capita in Europe ($1 850.1) in 8.8 times.

The growth of transportation in Ukraine was 6.6% in the 2000s, ranked 75th in the world. The growth of transportation in Ukraine (6.6%) was greater than growth of transportation in the world (3.9%), was greater than growth of transportation in Europe (3.1%).

Comparison with neighbors. The Ukraine's transportation was greater than in Hungary ($9.4 billion), in Bulgaria ($3.2 billion), in Belarus ($2.4 billion), and in Moldova ($348.9 million); but less than in Russia ($65.2 billion), in Poland ($27.1 billion), and in Romania

Chapter VII. Transportation

($12.1 billion). The value of transportation per capita in Ukraine was greater than in Moldova ($84.0); but less than in Hungary ($931.3), in Poland ($704.3), in Romania ($564.3), in Russia ($452.0), in Bulgaria ($418.8), and in Belarus ($249.7). The growth of transportation in Ukraine was greater than in Russia (4.7%), in Belarus (4.5%), in Poland (4.2%), and in Hungary (3.5%); but less than in Moldova (9.5%), in Bulgaria (7.4%), and in Romania (6.9%).

Comparison with leaders. The value of transportation in Ukraine was less than in the USA ($1.2 trillion), in Japan ($468.5 billion), in Germany ($228.2 billion), in the United Kingdom ($215.9 billion), and in France ($185.6 billion). The sector of transportation per capita in Ukraine was less than in the USA ($4.0 thousand), in Japan ($3.7 thousand), in the UK ($3.6 thousand), in France ($3.0 thousand), and in Germany ($2.8 thousand). The growth of transportation in Ukraine was greater than in Germany (3.4%), in the United Kingdom (3.1%), in the USA (3.1%), in France (2.7%), and in Japan (1.5%).

The 2010s

The transportation of Ukraine was $14.4 billion per year in the 2010s, ranked 54th in the world, and was on a par with Middle Africa ($14.6 billion). The share in the world was 0.23%, and 0.80% in Europe.

The share of transportation in the economy of Ukraine was 12.1% in the 2010s, ranked 31st in the world, and was on a par with Ivory Coast (12.1%), Nigeria (12.1%), Israel (12.1%).

The transportation per capita in Ukraine was $319.2 in the 2010s, ranked 128th in the world, and was on a par with Guyana ($327.1). The sector of transportation per capita in Ukraine was less than transportation per capita in the world ($864.8) in 2.7 times, and was less than transportation per capita in Europe ($2 422.4) in 7.6 times.

The growth of transportation in Ukraine was 1.4% in the 2010s, ranked 177th in the world. The growth of transportation in Ukraine (1.4%) was less than growth of transportation in the world (4.0%), was less than growth of transportation in Europe (2.6%).

Comparison with neighbors. The value added of transportation in Ukraine was 6.3% higher than in Hungary ($13.5 billion), 2.4 times higher than in Belarus ($6.0 billion), 2.5 times higher than in Bulgaria ($5.8 billion), and 16.4 times higher than in Moldova ($873.7 million); but 8.5 times lower than in Russia ($122.2 billion), 3.3 times lower than in Poland ($47.9 billion), and 34.8% lower than in Romania ($22.0 billion). The transportation per capita in Ukraine was 48.6% higher than in Moldova ($214.8); but 4.3 times lower than in Hungary ($1 378.2), 3.9 times lower than in Poland ($1 257.0), 3.5 times lower than in Romania ($1 103.0), 2.6 times lower than in Russia ($844.4), 2.5 times lower than in Bulgaria ($806.4), and 49.5% lower than in Belarus ($632.6). The growth of transportation in Ukraine was less than in Romania (6.1%), in Moldova (5.6%), in Poland (5.6%), in Belarus (5.4%), in Hungary (4.0%), in Bulgaria (2.7%), and in Russia (2.0%).

Comparison with leaders. The value added of transportation in Ukraine was 124.6 times lower than in the United States ($1.8 trillion), 36.9 times lower than in Japan ($529.8 billion), 32.4 times lower than in China ($464.2 billion), 20.9 times lower than in Germany ($300.0 billion), and 18.0 times lower than in the United Kingdom ($257.7 billion). The Ukraine's transportation per capita was 17.5 times lower than in the United States ($5.6 thousand), 13.0 times lower than in Japan ($4.1 thousand), 12.3 times lower than in the UK ($3.9 thousand), 11.5 times lower than in Germany ($3.7 thousand), and 3.6% lower than in China ($331.0). The growth of transportation in Ukraine was greater than in Japan (0.81%); but less than in China (7.5%), in the United States (5.1%), in the United Kingdom (2.8%), and in Germany (2.7%).

Chapter VIII. Trade

Wholesale, retail trade, restaurants and hotels (ISIC G-H)

The value added of trade in Ukraine grew from $4.5 billion per year in the 1990s to $20.3 billion per year in the 2010s, that is by $15.8 billion or 4.5 times. The change occurred at $13.7 billion due to a 3.1-fold increase in prices, as also at $2.6 billion due to a 1.7-fold increase in productivity, as well as at -$512.6 million due to the downfall in population. The average annual growth in trade is -1.2%. The minimum value of trade was in 1999 at $2.5 billion. The maximum value of trade was in 2013 at $27.8 billion.

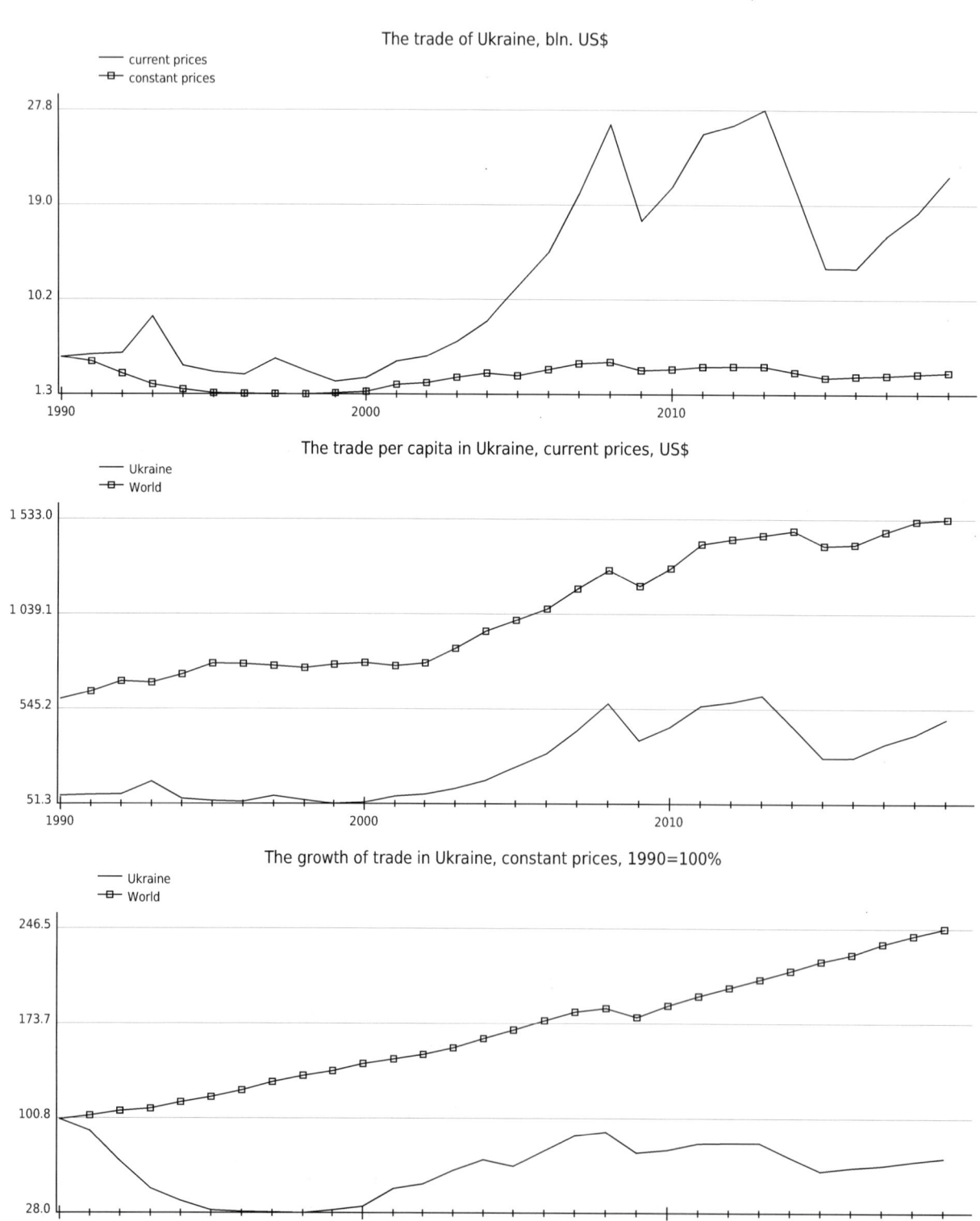

Chapter VIII. Trade

The 1990s

The value added of trade in Ukraine was $4.5 billion per year in the 1990s, ranked 55th in the world, and was on a par with Morocco ($4.5 billion). The share in the world was 0.11%, and 0.34% in Europe.

The share of trade in the economy of Ukraine was 7.5% in the 1990s, ranked 198th in the world, and was on a par with East Timor (7.5%).

The Ukraine's trade per capita was $88.4 in the 1990s, ranked 155th in the world, and was on a par with Georgia ($87.2), Central Asia ($89.9). The value of trade per capita in Ukraine was less than trade per capita in the world ($721.8) in 8.2 times, and was less than trade per capita in Europe ($1 798.1) in 20.3 times.

The growth of trade in Ukraine was -12.5% in the 1990s, ranked 205th in the world. The growth of trade in Ukraine (-12.5%) was less than growth of trade in the world (3.5%), was less than growth of trade in Europe (2.0%).

Comparison with neighbors. The trade of Ukraine was greater than in Hungary ($4.3 billion), in Romania ($3.5 billion), in Belarus ($1.4 billion), in Bulgaria ($1.2 billion), and in Moldova ($211.0 million); but less than in Russia ($73.9 billion) and in Poland ($21.0 billion). The sector of trade per capita in Ukraine was greater than in Moldova ($48.8); but less than in Poland ($547.6), in Russia ($499.6), in Hungary ($416.1), in Romania ($151.8), in Bulgaria ($142.0), and in Belarus ($140.7). The growth of trade in Ukraine was less than in Poland (4.8%), in Belarus (-0.85%), in Bulgaria (-1.3%), in Romania (-1.8%), in Hungary (-1.8%), in Russia (-1.9%), and in Moldova (-4.8%).

Comparison with leaders. The value of trade in Ukraine was less than in the USA ($1.2 trillion), in Japan ($713.2 billion), in Germany ($243.7 billion), in Italy ($185.6 billion), and in France ($177.0 billion). The trade per capita in Ukraine was less than in Japan ($5.7 thousand), in the USA ($4.4 thousand), in Italy ($3.3 thousand), in Germany ($3.0 thousand), and in France ($3.0 thousand). The growth of trade in Ukraine was less than in the United States (4.3%), in Japan (3.8%), in Germany (2.5%), in France (2.4%), and in Italy (1.9%).

The 2000s

The value of trade in Ukraine was $11.6 billion per year in the 2000s, ranked 47th in the world, and was on a par with New Zealand ($11.5 billion), Romania ($11.5 billion), Peru ($11.5 billion). The share in the world was 0.18%, and 0.58% in Europe.

The share of trade in the economy of Ukraine was 14.8% in the 2000s, ranked 107th in the world, and was on a par with Northern America (14.7%), Trinidad and Tobago (14.8%), Belgium (14.7%).

The value added of trade per capita in Ukraine was $246.8 in the 2000s, ranked 134th in the world, and was on a par with Jordan ($244.9), Tonga ($250.7), Morocco ($242.0). The value of trade per capita in Ukraine was less than trade per capita in the world ($990.3) in 4.0 times, and was less than trade per capita in Europe ($2 771.1) in 11.2 times.

The growth of trade in Ukraine was 9.4% in the 2000s, ranked 25th in the world. The growth of trade in Ukraine (9.4%) was greater than growth of trade in the world (2.7%), was greater than growth of trade in Europe (2.2%).

Comparison with neighbors. The value added of trade in Ukraine was greater than in Romania ($11.5 billion), in Hungary ($10.7 billion), in Bulgaria ($3.6 billion), in Belarus ($3.4 billion), and in Moldova ($478.6 million); but less than in Russia ($143.6 billion) and in Poland ($54.3 billion). The value of trade per capita in Ukraine was greater than in Moldova ($115.1); but less than in Poland ($1 412.2), in Hungary ($1 059.3), in Russia ($995.4), in Romania ($536.4), in Bulgaria ($462.7), and in Belarus ($353.1). The growth of trade in Ukraine was greater than in Russia (8.4%), in Romania (6.5%), in Bulgaria (5.6%), in Poland (3.6%), in Hungary (1.9%), and in Moldova (1.4%); but less than in Belarus (10.3%).

Comparison with leaders. The trade of Ukraine was less than in the USA ($1.9 trillion), in Japan ($771.8 billion), in Germany ($296.0 billion), in the United Kingdom ($293.5 billion), and in China ($262.0 billion). The value of trade per capita in Ukraine was greater than in China ($197.5); but less than in the USA ($6.4 thousand), in Japan ($6.0 thousand), in the United Kingdom ($4.9 thousand), and in Germany ($3.6 thousand). The growth of trade in Ukraine was greater than in Germany (1.7%), in the United Kingdom (1.3%), in the United States (1.1%), and in Japan (-0.77%); but less than in China (11.9%).

The 2010s

The Ukrainian trade was $20.3 billion per year in the 2010s, ranked 56th in the world, and was on a par with Cuba ($20.4 billion). The share in the world was 0.19%, and 0.75% in Europe.

The share of trade in the economy of Ukraine was 17.1% in the 2010s, ranked 80th in the world, and was on a par with Saint Kitts and Nevis (17.1%), Cyprus (17.2%), Micronesia (17.0%).

The Ukrainian trade per capita was $451.6 in the 2010s, ranked 142nd in the world, and was on a par with Nigeria ($454.3), Iraq ($455.2), Sri Lanka ($459.2). The trade per capita in Ukraine was less than trade per capita in the world ($1 436.8) in 3.2 times, and was less than trade per capita in Europe ($3 620.4) in 8.0 times.

The growth of trade in Ukraine was -0.6% in the 2010s, ranked 192nd in the world. The growth of trade in Ukraine (-0.59%) was less than growth of trade in the world (3.3%), was less than growth of trade in Europe (2.0%).

Comparison with neighbors. The sector of trade in Ukraine was 6.9% higher than in Romania ($19.0 billion), 44.4% higher than in Hungary ($14.1 billion), 2.6 times higher than in Bulgaria ($7.9 billion), 2.6 times higher than in Belarus ($7.8 billion), and 14.4 times higher than in Moldova ($1.4 billion); but 13.6 times lower than in Russia ($277.2 billion) and 4.4 times lower than in Poland ($89.4 billion). The sector of trade per capita in Ukraine was 30.7% higher than in Moldova ($345.5); but 5.2 times lower than in Poland ($2.3 thousand), 4.2 times lower than in Russia ($1 914.6), 3.2 times lower than in Hungary ($1 435.0), 2.4 times lower than in Bulgaria ($1 095.7), 2.1 times lower than in Romania ($952.6), and 45.6% lower than in Belarus ($830.0). The growth of trade in Ukraine was less than in Romania (8.1%), in Moldova (6.7%), in Bulgaria (4.8%), in Hungary (4.3%), in Belarus (4.1%), in Poland (3.2%), and in Russia (1.7%).

Comparison with leaders. The value added of trade in Ukraine was 128.8 times lower than in the USA ($2.6 trillion), 58.8 times lower than in China ($1.2 trillion), 42.8 times lower than in Japan ($869.5 billion), 18.3 times lower than in Germany ($372.6 billion), and 16.3 times lower than in the United Kingdom ($330.0 billion). The sector of trade per capita in Ukraine was 18.1 times lower than in the USA ($8.2 thousand), 15.1 times lower than in Japan ($6.8 thousand), 11.1 times lower than in the UK ($5.0 thousand), 10.1 times lower than in Germany ($4.6 thousand), and 47.0% lower than in China ($851.7). The growth of trade in Ukraine was less than in China (8.9%), in the UK (2.8%), in the United States (2.3%), in Germany (2.0%), and in Japan (0.77%).

Chapter IX. Services

(ISIC J-P)

The sector of services in Ukraine increased from $12.3 billion per year in the 1990s to $38.6 billion per year in the 2010s, that is by $26.3 billion or 3.1 times. The change occurred at $21.9 billion due to a 2.3-fold increase in prices, as also at $5.8 billion due to a 1.5-fold increase in productivity, as well as at -$1.4 billion due to the fall in population. The average annual growth in services is 1.0%. The minimum value of services was in 1999 at $6.0 billion. The maximum value of services was in 2013 at $56.0 billion.

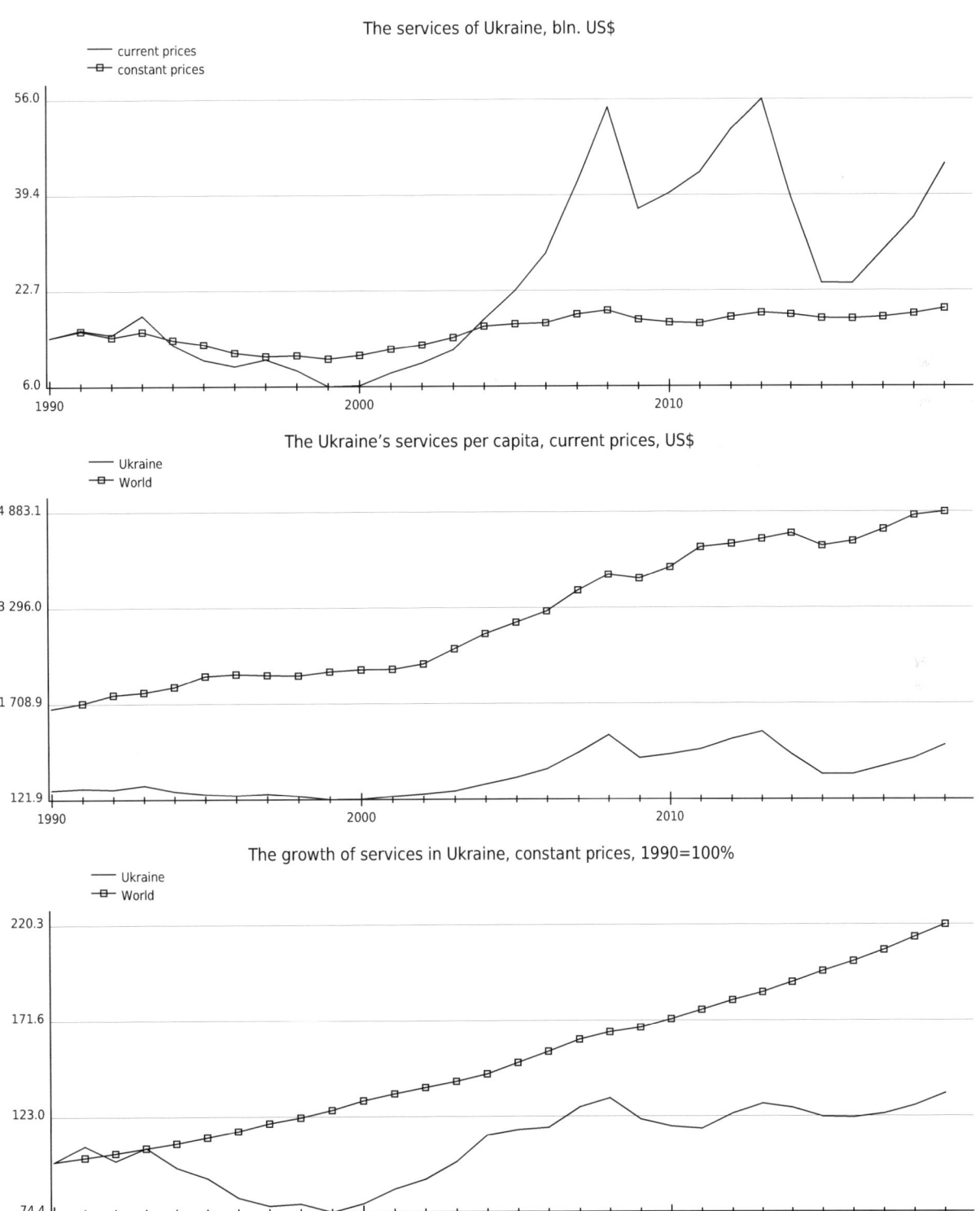

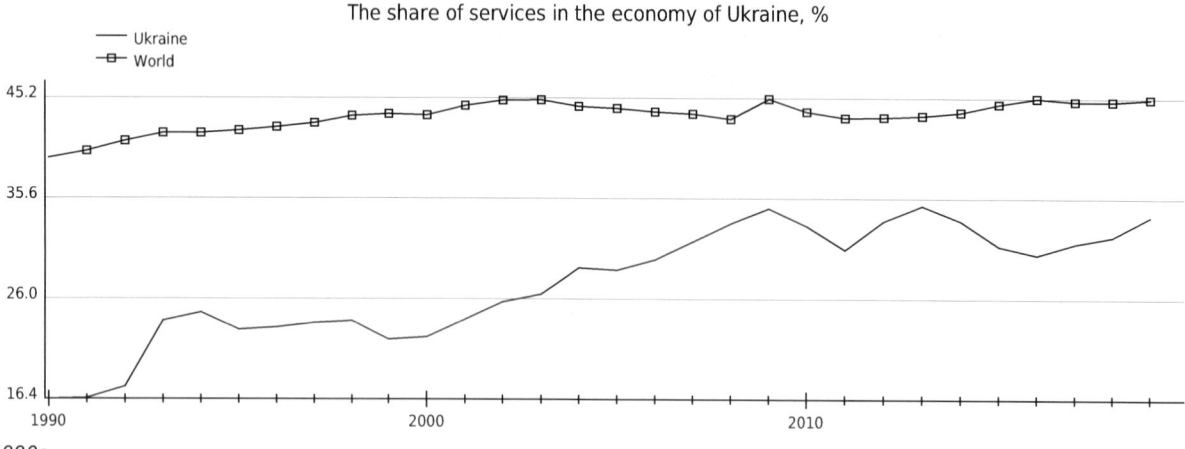

The 1990s

The Ukraine's services were $12.3 billion per year in the 1990s, ranked 51st in the world, and were on a par with Peru ($12.3 billion). The share in the world was 0.11%, and 0.32% in Europe.

The share of services in the economy of Ukraine was 20.5% in the 1990s, ranked 167th in the world, and was on a par with Middle Africa (20.4%).

The sector of services per capita in Ukraine was $241.9 in the 1990s, ranked 140th in the world, and was on a par with Cameroon ($242.4), the Solomon Islands ($240.1), Bolivia ($237.1). The value added of services per capita in Ukraine was less than services per capita in the world ($2 014.6) in 8.3 times, and was less than services per capita in Europe ($5 286.9) in 21.9 times.

The growth of services in Ukraine was -3.2% in the 1990s, ranked 194th in the world. The growth of services in Ukraine (-3.2%) was less than growth of services in the world (2.7%), was less than growth of services in Europe (2.1%).

Comparison with neighbors. The sector of services in Ukraine was greater than in Romania ($7.2 billion), in Bulgaria ($4.8 billion), in Belarus ($2.9 billion), and in Moldova ($502.4 million); but less than in Russia ($71.4 billion), in Poland ($33.5 billion), and in Hungary ($14.6 billion). The Ukraine's services per capita were greater than in Moldova ($116.1); but less than in Hungary ($1 408.7), in Poland ($873.3), in Bulgaria ($564.0), in Russia ($482.5), in Romania ($311.5), and in Belarus ($291.6). The growth of services in Ukraine was greater than in Belarus (-3.5%), in Bulgaria (-5.4%), and in Moldova (-7.5%); but less than in Romania (3.7%), in Poland (0.74%), in Hungary (0.63%), and in Russia (-1.2%).

Comparison with leaders. The Ukrainian services were less than in the United States ($3.8 trillion), in Japan ($1.6 trillion), in Germany ($908.0 billion), in France ($628.2 billion), and in the United Kingdom ($592.3 billion). The value added of services per capita in Ukraine was less than in the United States ($14.4 thousand), in Japan ($12.8 thousand), in Germany ($11.3 thousand), in France ($10.6 thousand), and in the United Kingdom ($10.2 thousand). The growth of services in Ukraine was less than in Germany (3.2%), in the United Kingdom (3.0%), in the United States (2.3%), in Japan (1.7%), and in France (1.6%).

The 2000s

The value of services in Ukraine was $24.0 billion per year in the 2000s, ranked 52nd in the world, and was on a par with Kuwait ($24.3 billion), Pakistan ($23.6 billion). The share in the world was 0.12%, and 0.37% in Europe.

The share of services in the economy of Ukraine was 30.3% in the 2000s, ranked 128th in the world, and was on a par with Kuwait (30.4%), the Comoros (30.2%).

The value added of services per capita in Ukraine was $507.4 in the 2000s, ranked 136th in the world, and was on a par with Kiribati ($501.9), Georgia ($499.1), China ($517.4). The value of services per capita in Ukraine was less than services per capita in the world ($3 011.2) in 5.9 times, and was less than services per capita in Europe ($8 787.5) in 17.3 times.

The growth of services in Ukraine was 5% in the 2000s, ranked 63rd in the world, and was on a par with Cameroon (5.0%), Venezuela (5.0%), Western Asia (5.0%). The growth of services in Ukraine (5.0%) was greater than growth of services in the world (2.9%), was greater than growth of services in Europe (2.0%).

Comparison with neighbors. The sector of services in Ukraine was greater than in Bulgaria ($9.8 billion), in Belarus ($6.7 billion), and

Chapter IX. Services

in Moldova ($1.1 billion); but less than in Russia ($195.9 billion), in Poland ($93.6 billion), in Hungary ($36.4 billion), and in Romania ($25.8 billion). The value of services per capita in Ukraine was greater than in Moldova ($270.0); but less than in Hungary ($3.6 thousand), in Poland ($2.4 thousand), in Russia ($1 357.8), in Bulgaria ($1 263.3), in Romania ($1 203.2), and in Belarus ($694.7). The growth of services in Ukraine was greater than in Bulgaria (4.5%), in Russia (4.3%), in Moldova (3.9%), in Belarus (3.9%), in Poland (3.9%), in Romania (3.1%), and in Hungary (2.3%).

Comparison with leaders. The services of Ukraine were less than in the United States ($6.7 trillion), in Japan ($2.0 trillion), in Germany ($1.2 trillion), in the United Kingdom ($1.1 trillion), and in France ($997.0 billion). The services per capita in Ukraine were less than in the United States ($22.9 thousand), in the United Kingdom ($18.0 thousand), in France ($15.9 thousand), in Japan ($15.3 thousand), and in Germany ($15.0 thousand). The growth of services in Ukraine was greater than in the United Kingdom (2.7%), in the United States (2.0%), in France (1.5%), in Japan (1.2%), and in Germany (0.57%).

The 2010s

The value of services in Ukraine was $38.6 billion per year in the 2010s, ranked 59th in the world. The share in the world was 0.12%, and 0.43% in Europe.

The share of services in the economy of Ukraine was 32.6% in the 2010s, ranked 123rd in the world, and was on a par with Panama (32.6%), Nicaragua (32.7%), Swaziland (32.8%).

The sector of services per capita in Ukraine was $859.0 in the 2010s, ranked 144th in the world, and was on a par with Northern Africa ($864.5). The sector of services per capita in Ukraine was less than services per capita in the world ($4 467.8) in 5.2 times, and was less than services per capita in Europe ($12 213.1) in 14.2 times.

The growth of services in Ukraine was 1% in the 2010s, ranked 175th in the world, and was on a par with the Federated States of Micronesia (1.0%). The growth of services in Ukraine (1.0%) was less than growth of services in the world (2.7%), was less than growth of services in Europe (1.3%).

Comparison with neighbors. The sector of services in Ukraine was 92.9% higher than in Bulgaria ($20.0 billion), 2.6 times higher than in Belarus ($14.9 billion), and 14.6 times higher than in Moldova ($2.6 billion); but 14.9 times lower than in Russia ($577.3 billion), 4.1 times lower than in Poland ($158.3 billion), 39.7% lower than in Romania ($64.1 billion), and 22.9% lower than in Hungary ($50.1 billion). The value of services per capita in Ukraine was 32.0% higher than in Moldova ($650.7); but 5.9 times lower than in Hungary ($5.1 thousand), 4.8 times lower than in Poland ($4.2 thousand), 4.6 times lower than in Russia ($4.0 thousand), 3.7 times lower than in Romania ($3.2 thousand), 3.2 times lower than in Bulgaria ($2.8 thousand), and 45.4% lower than in Belarus ($1 574.2). The growth of services in Ukraine was greater than in Bulgaria (0.78%) and in Belarus (-0.48%); but less than in Poland (3.1%), in Romania (2.6%), in Hungary (2.3%), in Russia (1.5%), and in Moldova (1.3%).

Comparison with leaders. The Ukrainian services were 257.8 times lower than in the USA ($10.0 trillion), 91.8 times lower than in China ($3.5 trillion), 58.9 times lower than in Japan ($2.3 trillion), 41.6 times lower than in Germany ($1.6 trillion), and 35.1 times lower than in the United Kingdom ($1.4 trillion). The services per capita in Ukraine were 36.3 times lower than in the USA ($31.2 thousand), 24.1 times lower than in the United Kingdom ($20.7 thousand), 22.9 times lower than in Germany ($19.6 thousand), 20.7 times lower than in Japan ($17.8 thousand), and 2.9 times lower than in China ($2.5 thousand). The growth of services in Ukraine was greater than in Japan (0.99%); but less than in China (8.4%), in the USA (1.8%), in the United Kingdom (1.7%), and in Germany (1.2%).

Part III. External relations

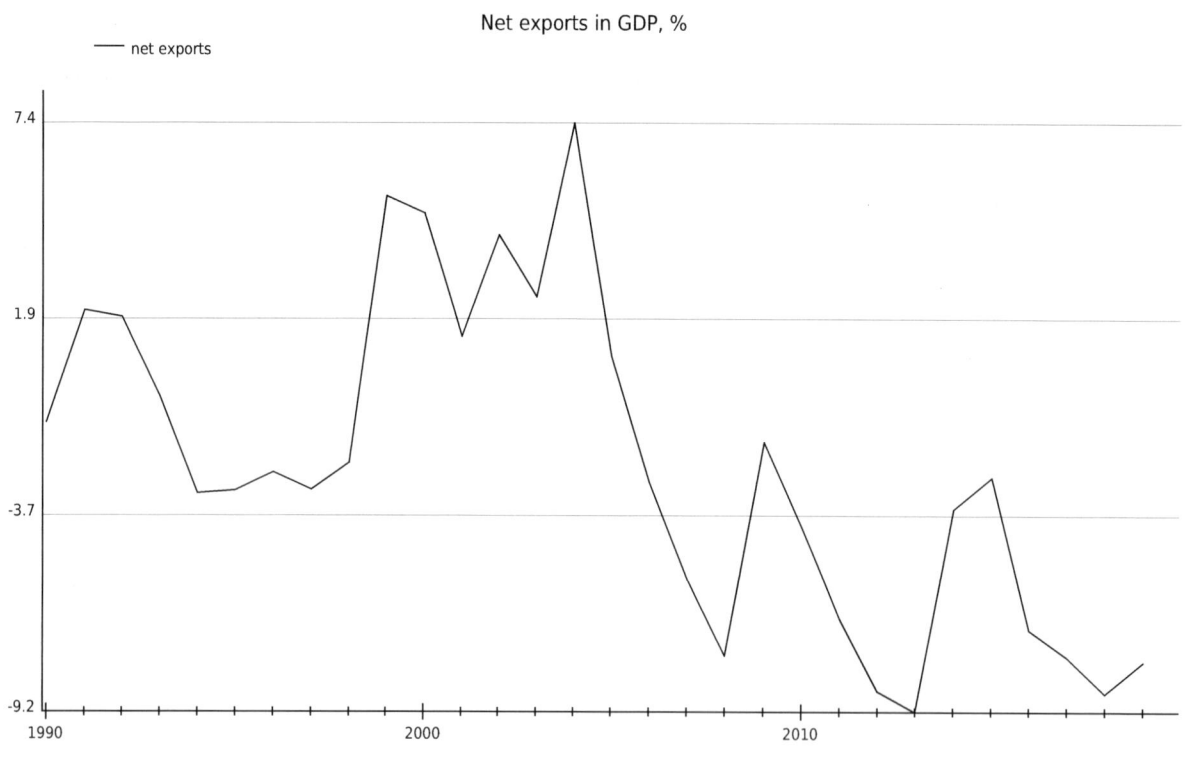

Chapter X. Exports

Exports of goods and services

The Ukraine's exports increased from $20.1 billion per year in the 1990s to $64.3 billion per year in the 2010s, that is by $44.2 billion or 3.2 times. The change occurred at $46.3 billion due to a 3.6-fold increase in prices, as also at $185.0 million due to a 1.0-fold increase in per capita rate, as well as at -$2.3 billion due to the fall in population. The average annual growth in exports is -2.8%. The minimum value of exports was in 1999 at $17.2 billion. The maximum value of exports was in 2012 at $83.9 billion.

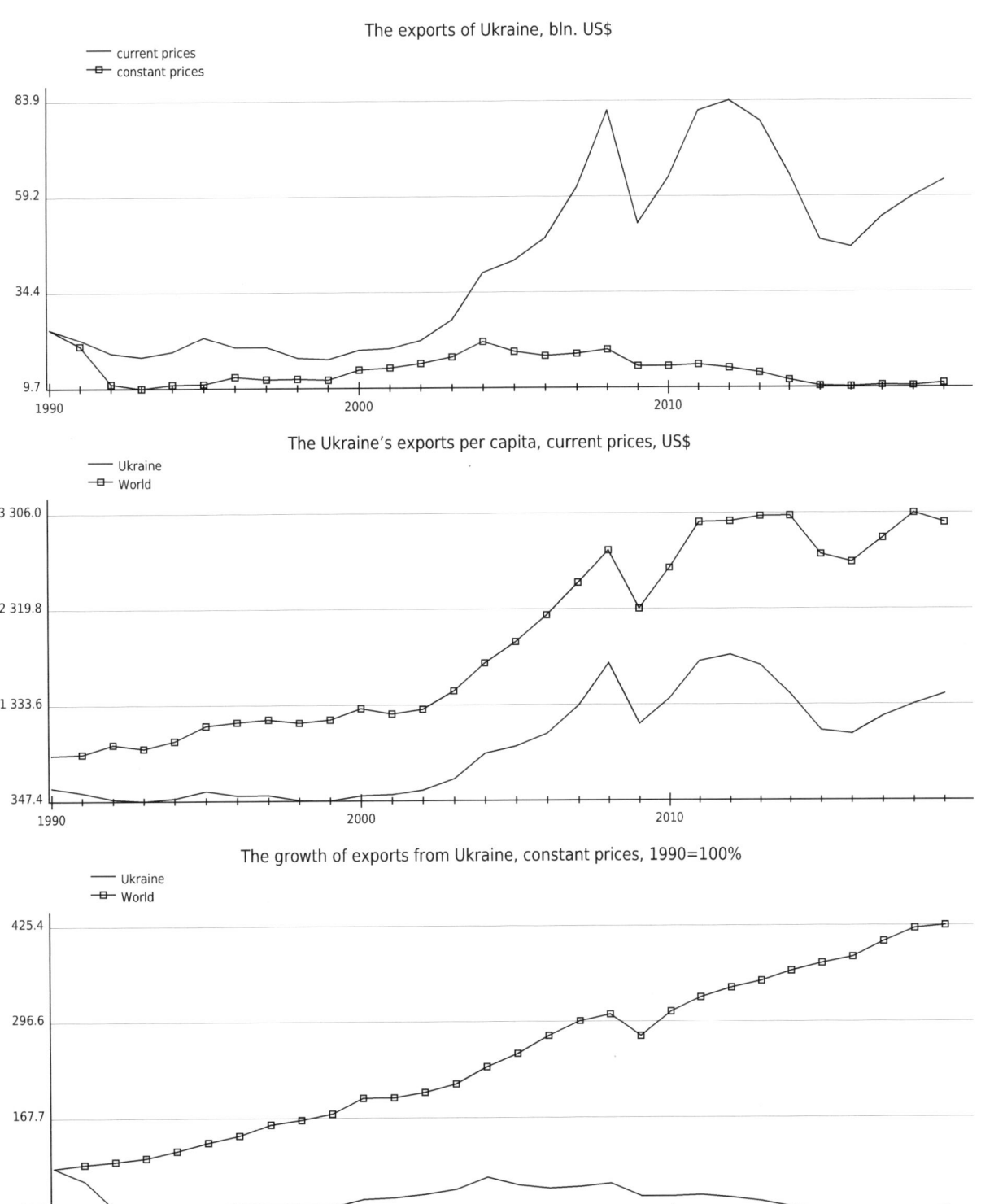

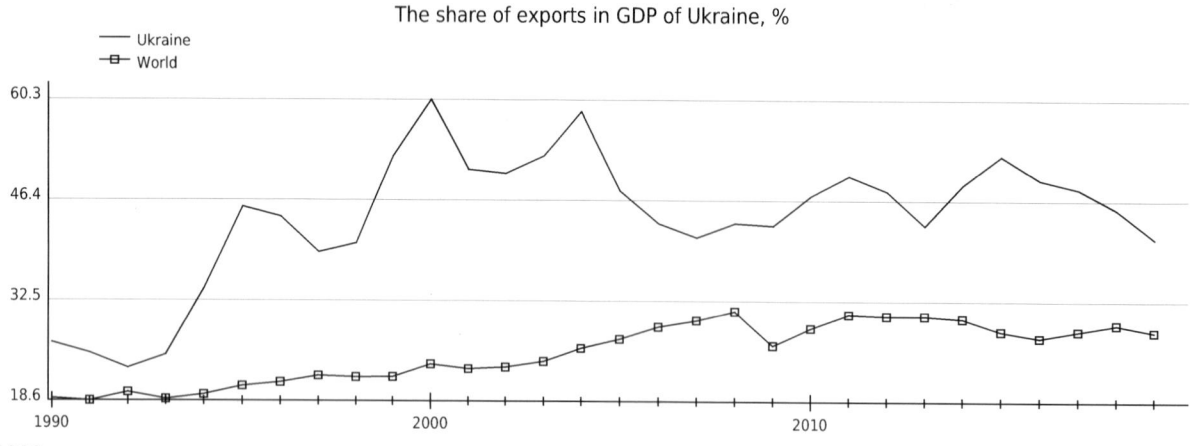

The 1990s

The Ukrainian exports were $20.1 billion per year in the 1990s, ranked 42nd in the world, and were on a par with Luxembourg ($20.0 billion), Venezuela ($19.9 billion), Czechia ($20.4 billion). The share in the world was 0.34%, and 0.73% from Europe.

The share of exports in GDP of Ukraine was 32.7% in the 1990s, ranked 95th in the world, and was on a par with Moldova (32.6%), Zambia (32.5%).

The exports per capita from Ukraine were $396.7 in the 1990s, ranked 125th in the world, and were on a par with Cuba ($404.7). The value of exports per capita from Ukraine was less than exports per capita in the world ($1 029.5) in 2.6 times, and was less than exports per capita from Europe ($3 810.5) in 9.6 times.

The growth of exports from Ukraine was -7.9% in the 1990s, ranked 197th in the world, and was on a par with DPRK (-7.9%). The growth of exports from Ukraine (-7.9%) was less than growth of exports in the world (6.9%), was less than growth of exports from Europe (6.5%).

Comparison with neighbors. The value of exports from Ukraine was greater than from Hungary ($16.4 billion), from Belarus ($8.7 billion), from Romania ($7.9 billion), from Bulgaria ($5.4 billion), and from Moldova ($873.0 million); but less than from Russia ($130.4 billion) and from Poland ($29.1 billion). The Ukraine's exports per capita were greater than from Romania ($343.0) and from Moldova ($201.7); but less than from Hungary ($1 583.8), from Russia ($881.8), from Belarus ($860.1), from Poland ($757.9), and from Bulgaria ($636.1). The growth of exports from Ukraine was greater than from Bulgaria (-14.8%); but less than from Russia (12.1%), from Poland (9.6%), from Hungary (8.5%), from Romania (-0.13%), from Moldova (-5.7%), and from Belarus (-7.2%).

Comparison with leaders. The value of exports from Ukraine was less than from the United States ($773.6 billion), from Germany ($509.0 billion), from Japan ($418.7 billion), from France ($329.8 billion), and from the United Kingdom ($324.3 billion). The exports per capita from Ukraine were less than from Germany ($6.3 thousand), from the UK ($5.6 thousand), from France ($5.6 thousand), from Japan ($3.3 thousand), and from the United States ($2.9 thousand). The growth of exports from Ukraine was less than from the USA (7.2%), from France (6.5%), from Germany (6.0%), from the United Kingdom (5.7%), and from Japan (4.2%).

The 2000s

The value of exports from Ukraine was $41.4 billion per year in the 2000s, ranked 50th in the world, and was on a par with Algeria ($42.3 billion). The share in the world was 0.33%, and 0.74% from Europe.

The structure of exports: primary products (11.7%), resource-based manufactures (23.0%), low technology manufactures (24.1%), medium technology manufactures (35.0%), and high technology manufactures (4.2%).

Ukraine exported goods to Russia (22.3%), Turkey (6.3%), Italy (5.0%), Germany (3.9%), Poland (3.2%) and other countries (59.4%).

The share of exports in GDP of Ukraine was 46.3% in the 2000s, ranked 72nd in the world.

The Ukraine's exports per capita were $877.5 in the 2000s, ranked 120th in the world, and were on a par with Cabo Verde ($871.4), Bosnia and Herzegovina ($863.2), Central Asia ($858.1). The value of exports per capita from Ukraine was less than exports per capita in the world ($1 933.7) in 2.2 times, and was less than exports per capita from Europe ($7 642.0) in 8.7 times.

The growth of exports from Ukraine was 2.5% in the 2000s, ranked 148th in the world, and was on a par with Eritrea (2.5%), Mexico

Chapter X. Exports

(2.6%). The growth of exports from Ukraine (2.5%) was less than growth of exports in the world (4.8%), was less than growth of exports from Europe (3.8%).

Comparison with neighbors. The Ukrainian exports were greater than from Romania ($28.9 billion), from Belarus ($18.2 billion), from Bulgaria ($13.6 billion), and from Moldova ($1.2 billion); but less than from Russia ($256.1 billion), from Poland ($108.3 billion), and from Hungary ($70.4 billion). The Ukraine's exports per capita were greater than from Moldova ($290.8); but less than from Hungary ($7.0 thousand), from Poland ($2.8 thousand), from Belarus ($1 888.1), from Russia ($1 774.6), from Bulgaria ($1 759.9), and from Romania ($1 346.2). The growth of exports from Ukraine was less than from Hungary (10.4%), from Moldova (8.9%), from Poland (8.4%), from Romania (7.9%), from Russia (6.3%), from Belarus (6.2%), and from Bulgaria (4.4%).

Comparison with leaders. The exports of Ukraine were less than from the USA ($1.3 trillion), from Germany ($1.0 trillion), from China ($780.2 billion), from Japan ($626.3 billion), and from the United Kingdom ($591.1 billion). The value of exports per capita from Ukraine was greater than from China ($588.1); but less than from Germany ($12.8 thousand), from the UK ($9.8 thousand), from Japan ($4.9 thousand), and from the USA ($4.5 thousand). The growth of exports from Ukraine was less than from China (12.7%), from Germany (5.0%), from Japan (3.5%), from the United States (3.3%), and from the United Kingdom (2.8%).

The 2010s

The exports of Ukraine were $64.3 billion per year in the 2010s, ranked 54th in the world. The share in the world was 0.28%, and 0.72% from Europe.

The structure of exports: primary products (20.8%), resource-based manufactures (27.1%), low technology manufactures (17.3%), medium technology manufactures (29.1%), and high technology manufactures (4.2%).

Ukraine exported goods to Russia (19.5%), Turkey (5.9%), Poland (4.8%), Italy (4.6%), China (4.1%) and other countries (61.1%).

The share of exports in GDP of Ukraine was 46.8% in the 2010s, ranked 71st in the world, and was on a par with Mauritius (46.8%).

The Ukrainian exports per capita were $1 430.2 in the 2010s, ranked 131st in the world, and were on a par with Iran ($1 436.9), Cuba ($1 413.8), Papua New Guinea ($1 395.6). The Ukrainian exports per capita were less than exports per capita in the world ($3 098.9) in 2.2 times, and were less than exports per capita from Europe ($12 067.8) in 8.4 times.

The growth of exports from Ukraine was -3.4% in the 2010s, ranked 201st in the world. The growth of exports from Ukraine (-3.4%) was less than growth of exports in the world (4.4%), was less than growth of exports from Europe (4.4%).

Comparison with neighbors. The value of exports from Ukraine was 60.6% higher than from Belarus ($40.0 billion), 79.5% higher than from Bulgaria ($35.8 billion), and 22.5 times higher than from Moldova ($2.9 billion); but 7.6 times lower than from Russia ($488.7 billion), 4.0 times lower than from Poland ($255.2 billion), 46.0% lower than from Hungary ($119.1 billion), and 18.0% lower than from Romania ($78.4 billion). The value of exports per capita from Ukraine was 2.0 times higher than from Moldova ($702.8); but 8.5 times lower than from Hungary ($12.2 thousand), 4.7 times lower than from Poland ($6.7 thousand), 3.5 times lower than from Bulgaria ($5.0 thousand), 3.0 times lower than from Belarus ($4.2 thousand), 2.7 times lower than from Romania ($3.9 thousand), and 2.4 times lower than from Russia ($3.4 thousand). The growth of exports from Ukraine was less than from Romania (9.4%), from Moldova (8.9%), from Poland (7.6%), from Bulgaria (6.2%), from Hungary (5.7%), from Belarus (5.0%), and from Russia (2.9%).

Comparison with leaders. The exports of Ukraine were 35.7 times lower than from China ($2.3 trillion), 35.3 times lower than from the United States ($2.3 trillion), 26.2 times lower than from Germany ($1.7 trillion), 13.4 times lower than from Japan ($859.4 billion), and 12.7 times lower than from the United Kingdom ($815.1 billion). The Ukraine's exports per capita were 14.4 times lower than from Germany ($20.6 thousand), 8.7 times lower than from the UK ($12.4 thousand), 5.0 times lower than from the United States ($7.1 thousand), 4.7 times lower than from Japan ($6.7 thousand), and 12.5% lower than from China ($1 635.3). The growth of exports from Ukraine was less than from China (6.8%), from Germany (4.7%), from Japan (4.6%), from the United States (3.7%), and from the UK (3.1%).

Chapter XI. Imports

Imports of goods and services

The imports of Ukraine grew from $20.4 billion per year in the 1990s to $73.7 billion per year in the 2010s, that is by $53.3 billion or 3.6 times. The change occurred at $45.5 billion due to a 2.6-fold increase in prices, as also at $10.1 billion due to a 1.6-fold increase in per capita rate, as well as at -$2.3 billion due to the decline in population. The average annual growth in imports is -1.5%. The minimum value of imports was in 1999 at $15.4 billion. The maximum value of imports was in 2012 at $99.1 billion.

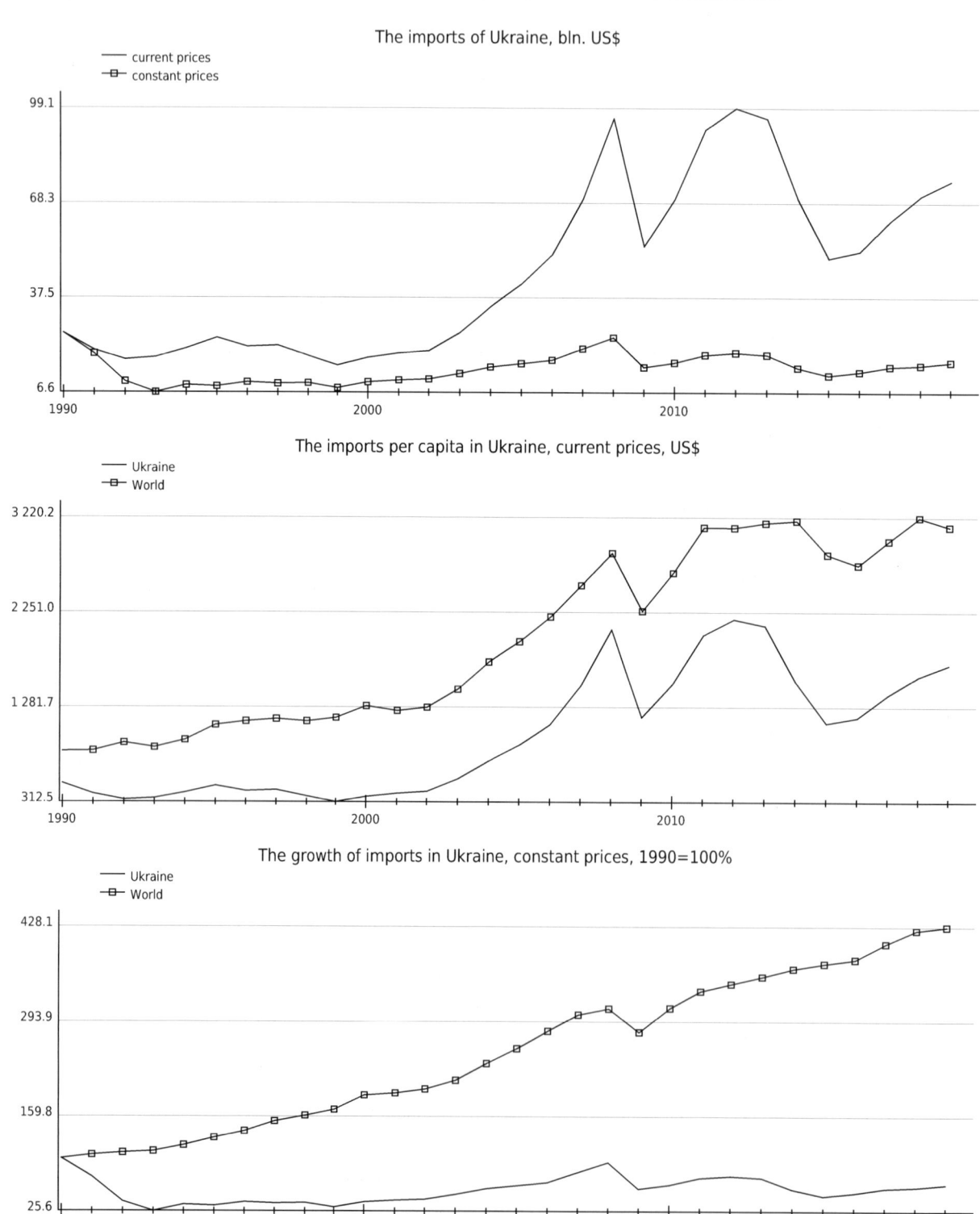

Chapter XI. Imports

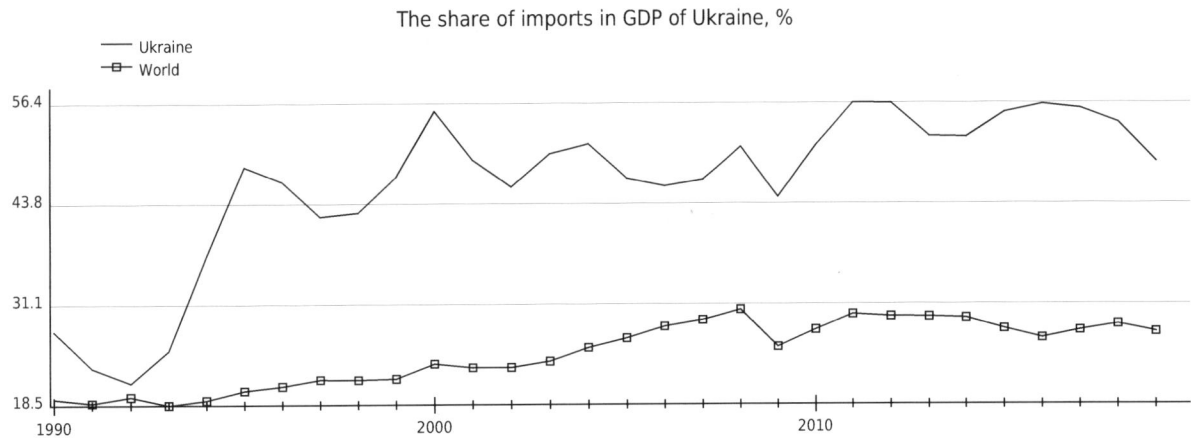

The 1990s

The imports of Ukraine were $20.4 billion per year in the 1990s, ranked 43rd in the world, and were on a par with Central Asia ($20.0 billion), Czechia ($20.9 billion). The share in the world was 0.35%, and 0.77% in Europe.

The share of imports in GDP of Ukraine was 33.2% in the 1990s, ranked 130th in the world, and was on a par with Iceland (33.3%), Macedonia (33.4%).

The imports per capita in Ukraine were $402.3 in the 1990s, ranked 141st in the world, and were on a par with the Comoros ($410.6), Serbia ($394.0). The value of imports per capita in Ukraine was less than imports per capita in the world ($1 015.5) in 2.5 times, and was less than imports per capita in Europe ($3 655.2) in 9.1 times.

The growth of imports in Ukraine was -12.1% in the 1990s, ranked 203rd in the world, and was on a par with Central Asia (-12.2%). The growth of imports in Ukraine (-12.1%) was less than growth of imports in the world (6.6%), was less than growth of imports in Europe (5.9%).

Comparison with neighbors. The Ukrainian imports were greater than in Hungary ($17.0 billion), in Romania ($9.9 billion), in Belarus ($9.3 billion), in Bulgaria ($4.5 billion), and in Moldova ($1.2 billion); but less than in Russia ($108.7 billion) and in Poland ($30.7 billion). The imports per capita in Ukraine were greater than in Moldova ($268.4); but less than in Hungary ($1 641.4), in Belarus ($922.5), in Poland ($801.3), in Russia ($735.2), in Bulgaria ($534.4), and in Romania ($430.2). The growth of imports in Ukraine was greater than in Bulgaria (-16.5%); but less than in Poland (13.1%), in Hungary (10.9%), in Romania (3.7%), in Russia (2.9%), in Moldova (-2.3%), and in Belarus (-10.2%).

Comparison with leaders. The value of imports in Ukraine was less than in the USA ($874.1 billion), in Germany ($501.6 billion), in Japan ($355.9 billion), in the United Kingdom ($330.2 billion), and in France ($308.5 billion). The imports per capita in Ukraine were less than in Germany ($6.2 thousand), in the UK ($5.7 thousand), in France ($5.2 thousand), in the USA ($3.3 thousand), and in Japan ($2.8 thousand). The growth of imports in Ukraine was less than in the United States (8.3%), in Germany (6.4%), in France (5.1%), in the UK (5.1%), and in Japan (3.3%).

The 2000s

The imports of Ukraine were $43.1 billion per year in the 2000s, ranked 45th in the world, and were on a par with Vietnam ($43.2 billion). The share in the world was 0.35%, and 0.81% in Europe.

The structure of imports: primary products (31.5%), resource-based manufactures (17.1%), low technology manufactures (9.7%), medium technology manufactures (31.1%), and high technology manufactures (8.9%).

Ukraine imported goods from Russia (27.6%), Germany (10.8%), Turkmenistan (7.0%), Poland (6.8%), China (6.4%) and other countries (41.4%).

The share of imports in GDP of Ukraine was 48.2% in the 2000s, ranked 93rd in the world, and was on a par with Tunisia (48.4%), Turkmenistan (48.4%), Togo (48.4%).

The value of imports per capita in Ukraine was $912.6 in the 2000s, ranked 131st in the world, and was on a par with Asia ($898.2). The Ukraine's imports per capita were less than imports per capita in the world ($1 899.9) in 2.1 times, and were less than imports per capita in Europe ($7 287.7) in 8.0 times.

The growth of imports in Ukraine was 6.3% in the 2000s, ranked 81st in the world, and was on a par with Turkey (6.2%), Liberia (6.3%), Poland (6.4%). The growth of imports in Ukraine (6.3%) was greater than growth of imports in the world (5.1%), was greater than growth of imports in Europe (4.0%).

Comparison with neighbors. The Ukrainian imports were greater than in Romania ($39.6 billion), in Belarus ($20.0 billion), in Bulgaria ($17.8 billion), and in Moldova ($2.5 billion); but less than in Russia ($172.4 billion), in Poland ($118.2 billion), and in Hungary ($71.2 billion). The imports per capita in Ukraine were greater than in Moldova ($597.3); but less than in Hungary ($7.1 thousand), in Poland ($3.1 thousand), in Bulgaria ($2.3 thousand), in Belarus ($2.1 thousand), in Romania ($1 846.1), and in Russia ($1 194.9). The growth of imports in Ukraine was less than in Russia (14.0%), in Romania (13.4%), in Moldova (10.6%), in Belarus (9.5%), in Hungary (8.9%), in Bulgaria (7.7%), and in Poland (6.4%).

Comparison with leaders. The Ukrainian imports were less than in the United States ($1.9 trillion), in Germany ($914.7 billion), in the UK ($641.8 billion), in China ($641.1 billion), and in Japan ($566.4 billion). The Ukrainian imports per capita were greater than in China ($483.3); but less than in Germany ($11.2 thousand), in the UK ($10.6 thousand), in the USA ($6.4 thousand), and in Japan ($4.4 thousand). The growth of imports in Ukraine was greater than in Germany (3.7%), in the UK (3.1%), in the USA (2.8%), and in Japan (1.8%); but less than in China (15.1%).

The 2010s

The Ukrainian imports were $73.7 billion per year in the 2010s, ranked 49th in the world. The share in the world was 0.33%, and 0.89% in Europe.

The structure of imports: primary products (26.3%), resource-based manufactures (20.9%), low technology manufactures (10.9%), medium technology manufactures (29.5%), and high technology manufactures (11.3%).

Ukraine imported goods from Russia (19.6%), China (9.9%), Germany (9.9%), Poland (7.7%), Belarus (6.2%) and other countries (46.7%).

The share of imports in GDP of Ukraine was 53.7% in the 2010s, ranked 81st in the world, and was on a par with Samoa (53.7%), Kosovo (53.4%), Guinea (54.0%).

The imports per capita in Ukraine were $1 639.3 in the 2010s, ranked 134th in the world, and were on a par with Palestine ($1 636.6). The value of imports per capita in Ukraine was less than imports per capita in the world ($3 015.6) by 45.6%, and was less than imports per capita in Europe ($11 149.4) in 6.8 times.

The growth of imports in Ukraine was 1% in the 2010s, ranked 179th in the world, and was on a par with Antigua and Barbuda (1.0%). The growth of imports in Ukraine (1.0%) was less than growth of imports in the world (4.4%), was less than growth of imports in Europe (4.3%).

Comparison with neighbors. The Ukraine's imports were 80.7% higher than in Belarus ($40.8 billion), 2.1 times higher than in Bulgaria ($35.2 billion), and 13.5 times higher than in Moldova ($5.5 billion); but 4.9 times lower than in Russia ($364.2 billion), 3.3 times lower than in Poland ($246.8 billion), 33.3% lower than in Hungary ($110.6 billion), and 12.3% lower than in Romania ($84.1 billion). The Ukrainian imports per capita were 22.3% higher than in Moldova ($1 340.7); but 6.9 times lower than in Hungary ($11.3 thousand), 4.0 times lower than in Poland ($6.5 thousand), 3.0 times lower than in Bulgaria ($4.9 thousand), 2.6 times lower than in Belarus ($4.3 thousand), 2.6 times lower than in Romania ($4.2 thousand), and 34.9% lower than in Russia ($2.5 thousand). The growth of imports in Ukraine was less than in Romania (9.0%), in Moldova (6.8%), in Poland (6.6%), in Hungary (5.8%), in Bulgaria (4.9%), in Belarus (4.8%), and in Russia (3.5%).

Comparison with leaders. The value of imports in Ukraine was 38.2 times lower than in the United States ($2.8 trillion), 28.1 times lower than in China ($2.1 trillion), 19.7 times lower than in Germany ($1.5 trillion), 11.9 times lower than in Japan ($877.9 billion), and 11.6 times lower than in the UK ($854.8 billion). The imports per capita in Ukraine were 11.1% higher than in China ($1 475.4); but 10.8 times lower than in Germany ($17.8 thousand), 7.9 times lower than in the UK ($13.0 thousand), 5.4 times lower than in the USA ($8.8 thousand), and 4.2 times lower than in Japan ($6.9 thousand). The growth of imports in Ukraine was less than in China (8.2%), in Germany (4.8%), in the United States (4.4%), in Japan (3.8%), and in the UK (3.6%).

Part IV. Consumption

Chapter XII. Government consumption expenditure

General government final consumption expenditure

The government expenditure of Ukraine rose from $11.2 billion per year in the 1990s to $26.2 billion per year in the 2010s, that is by $15.0 billion or 2.3 times. The change occurred at $15.4 billion due to a 2.4-fold increase in prices, as also at $898.2 million due to a 1.1-fold increase in per capita rate, as well as at -$1.3 billion due to the decline in population. The average annual growth in public expenditure is -0.45%. The minimum value of government expenditure was in 2000 at $5.8 billion. The maximum value of government expenditure was in 2013 at $34.1 billion.

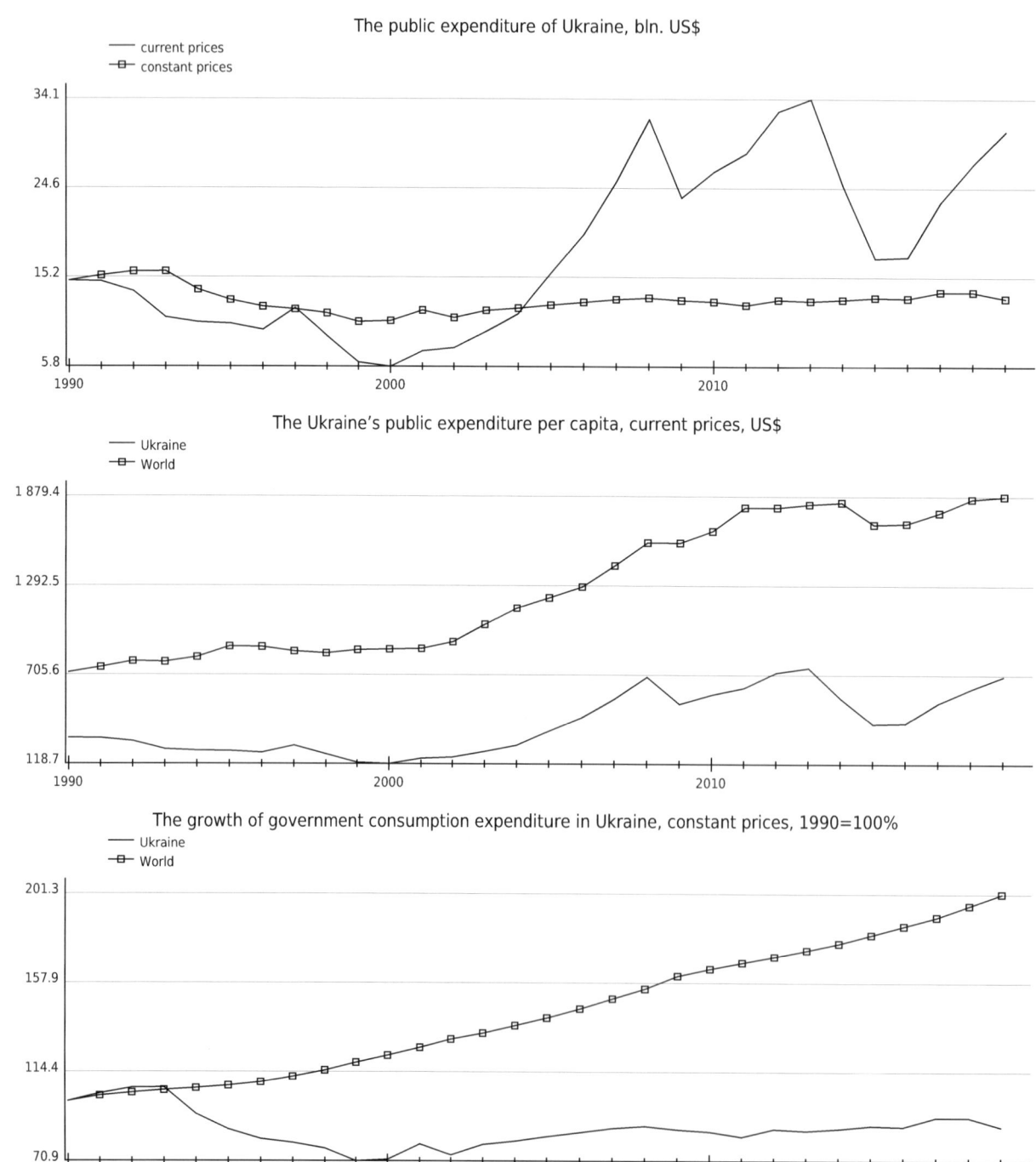

Chapter XII. Government consumption expenditure

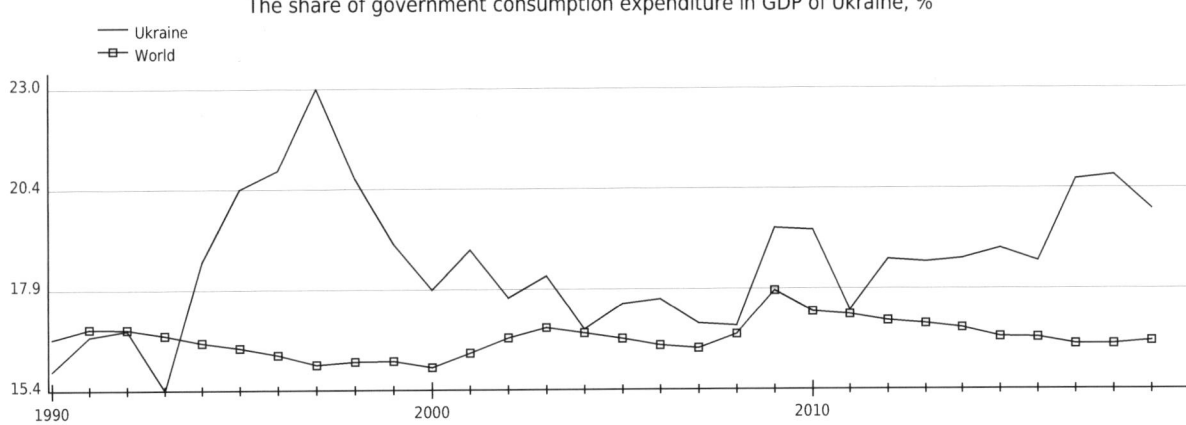

The 1990s

The Ukraine's public expenditure was $11.2 billion per year in the 1990s, ranked 36th in the world, and was on a par with Ireland ($11.5 billion). The share in the world was 0.24%, and 0.59% in Europe.

The share of public expenditure in GDP of Ukraine was 18.2% in the 1990s, ranked 76th in the world, and was on a par with Australia (18.1%), Oceania (18.3%), Southern Europe (18.1%).

The government consumption expenditure per capita in Ukraine was $220.3 in the 1990s, ranked 130th in the world. The Ukraine's government expenditure per capita was less than public expenditure per capita in the world ($824.8) in 3.7 times, and was less than public expenditure per capita in Europe ($2 620.7) in 11.9 times.

The growth of government expenditure in Ukraine was -3.8% in the 1990s, ranked 190th in the world. The growth of government consumption expenditure in Ukraine (-3.8%) was less than growth of public expenditure in the world (2.0%), was less than growth of government expenditure in Europe (1.3%).

Comparison with neighbors. The government expenditure of Ukraine was greater than in Hungary ($10.0 billion), in Romania ($4.5 billion), in Belarus ($3.1 billion), in Bulgaria ($2.0 billion), and in Moldova ($416.1 million); but less than in Russia ($74.6 billion) and in Poland ($24.6 billion). The public expenditure per capita in Ukraine was greater than in Romania ($193.6) and in Moldova ($96.2); but less than in Hungary ($968.5), in Poland ($640.8), in Russia ($504.2), in Belarus ($312.3), and in Bulgaria ($240.8). The growth of government expenditure in Ukraine was greater than in Bulgaria (-6.2%) and in Moldova (-6.5%); but less than in Romania (5.5%), in Poland (3.5%), in Hungary (-1.3%), in Russia (-2.7%), and in Belarus (-3.0%).

Comparison with leaders. The public expenditure of Ukraine was less than in the USA ($1.1 trillion), in Japan ($651.8 billion), in Germany ($419.6 billion), in France ($325.4 billion), and in the United Kingdom ($234.6 billion). The Ukrainian public expenditure per capita was less than in France ($5.5 thousand), in Germany ($5.2 thousand), in Japan ($5.2 thousand), in the United States ($4.3 thousand), and in the United Kingdom ($4.1 thousand). The growth of public expenditure in Ukraine was less than in Japan (3.0%), in Germany (2.4%), in the United Kingdom (2.1%), in France (1.8%), and in the USA (1.3%).

The 2000s

The Ukrainian public expenditure was $15.8 billion per year in the 2000s, ranked 44th in the world, and was on a par with Cuba ($15.6 billion). The share in the world was 0.20%, and 0.52% in Europe.

The share of public expenditure in GDP of Ukraine was 17.7% in the 2000s, ranked 76th in the world, and was on a par with Morocco (17.7%), Australasia (17.6%), Antigua and Barbuda (17.8%).

The Ukrainian government expenditure per capita was $335.0 in the 2000s, ranked 133rd in the world, and was on a par with the Dominican Republic ($339.5), Ecuador ($329.2). The Ukraine's government expenditure per capita was less than public expenditure per capita in the world ($1 200.9) in 3.6 times, and was less than government expenditure per capita in Europe ($4 171.1) in 12.5 times.

The growth of government expenditure in Ukraine was 2% in the 2000s, ranked 155th in the world, and was on a par with Belgium (2.0%), Denmark (2.0%). The growth of government consumption expenditure in Ukraine (2.0%) was less than growth of government expenditure in the world (3.1%), was less than growth of government consumption expenditure in Europe (2.1%).

Comparison with neighbors. The Ukrainian government expenditure was greater than in Belarus ($5.6 billion), in Bulgaria ($5.5 billion), and in Moldova ($601.1 million); but less than in Russia ($136.2 billion), in Poland ($57.2 billion), in Hungary ($22.1 billion), and in Romania ($16.8 billion). The Ukraine's public expenditure per capita was greater than in Moldova ($144.6); but less than in Hungary ($2.2 thousand), in Poland ($1 488.7), in Russia ($943.7), in Romania ($781.7), in Bulgaria ($711.6), and in Belarus ($583.1). The growth of government consumption expenditure in Ukraine was greater than in Russia (1.7%), in Bulgaria (1.7%), in Belarus (0.96%), and in Romania (-1.2%); but less than in Poland (4.1%), in Moldova (3.2%), and in Hungary (2.3%).

Comparison with leaders. The Ukraine's public expenditure was less than in the USA ($1.9 trillion), in Japan ($844.2 billion), in Germany ($520.1 billion), in France ($479.9 billion), and in the United Kingdom ($453.4 billion). The Ukraine's government consumption expenditure per capita was less than in France ($7.6 thousand), in the UK ($7.5 thousand), in Japan ($6.6 thousand), in the USA ($6.5 thousand), and in Germany ($6.4 thousand). The growth of government expenditure in Ukraine was greater than in Japan (1.7%), in France (1.7%), and in Germany (1.4%); but less than in the UK (2.9%) and in the United States (2.2%).

The 2010s

The public expenditure of Ukraine was $26.2 billion per year in the 2010s, ranked 56th in the world. The share in the world was 0.20%, and 0.62% in Europe.

The share of government expenditure in GDP of Ukraine was 19.1% in the 2010s, ranked 72nd in the world, and was on a par with Tunisia (19.1%), Burundi (18.9%), Samoa (19.2%).

The Ukraine's government consumption expenditure per capita was $582.8 in the 2010s, ranked 139th in the world, and was on a par with El Salvador ($585.6), Morocco ($593.5). The Ukraine's government expenditure per capita was less than government consumption expenditure per capita in the world ($1 785.1) in 3.1 times, and was less than public expenditure per capita in Europe ($5 705.5) in 9.8 times.

The growth of government expenditure in Ukraine was 0.2% in the 2010s, ranked 179th in the world. The growth of government expenditure in Ukraine (0.17%) was less than growth of government consumption expenditure in the world (2.3%), was less than growth of government consumption expenditure in Europe (0.99%).

Comparison with neighbors. The government consumption expenditure of Ukraine was 2.8 times higher than in Bulgaria ($9.4 billion), 2.9 times higher than in Belarus ($9.1 billion), and 18.6 times higher than in Moldova ($1.4 billion); but 12.2 times lower than in Russia ($320.0 billion), 3.6 times lower than in Poland ($94.8 billion), 13.2% lower than in Romania ($30.2 billion), and 6.7% lower than in Hungary ($28.1 billion). The public expenditure per capita in Ukraine was 68.2% higher than in Moldova ($346.6); but 4.9 times lower than in Hungary ($2.9 thousand), 4.3 times lower than in Poland ($2.5 thousand), 3.8 times lower than in Russia ($2.2 thousand), 2.6 times lower than in Romania ($1 514.3), 2.2 times lower than in Bulgaria ($1 300.0), and 39.8% lower than in Belarus ($967.4). The growth of public expenditure in Ukraine was greater than in Belarus (-0.56%) and in Moldova (-0.64%); but less than in Poland (2.4%), in Bulgaria (2.2%), in Romania (1.9%), in Hungary (1.7%), and in Russia (0.51%).

Comparison with leaders. The government expenditure of Ukraine was 101.2 times lower than in the United States ($2.7 trillion), 64.1 times lower than in China ($1.7 trillion), 39.8 times lower than in Japan ($1.0 trillion), 27.5 times lower than in Germany ($721.6 billion), and 24.3 times lower than in France ($637.9 billion). The Ukraine's public expenditure per capita was 16.5 times lower than in France ($9.6 thousand), 15.1 times lower than in Germany ($8.8 thousand), 14.2 times lower than in the United States ($8.3 thousand), 14.0 times lower than in Japan ($8.2 thousand), and 2.1 times lower than in China ($1 197.3). The growth of public expenditure in Ukraine was greater than in the United States (0.0052%); but less than in China (8.3%), in Germany (1.9%), in Japan (1.3%), and in France (1.3%).

Chapter XIII. Household consumption expenditure

(including Non-profit institutions serving households)

The Ukraine's household consumption expenditure enlarged from $33.4 billion per year in the 1990s to $94.9 billion per year in the 2010s, that is by $61.6 billion or 2.8 times. The change occurred at $28.1 billion due to a 1.4-fold increase in prices, as also at $37.3 billion due to a 2.3-fold increase in per capita rate, as well as at -$3.8 billion due to the decline in population. The average annual growth in household expenditure is 1.4%. The minimum value of household expenditure was in 2000 at $18.6 billion. The maximum value of household consumption expenditure was in 2013 at $132.3 billion.

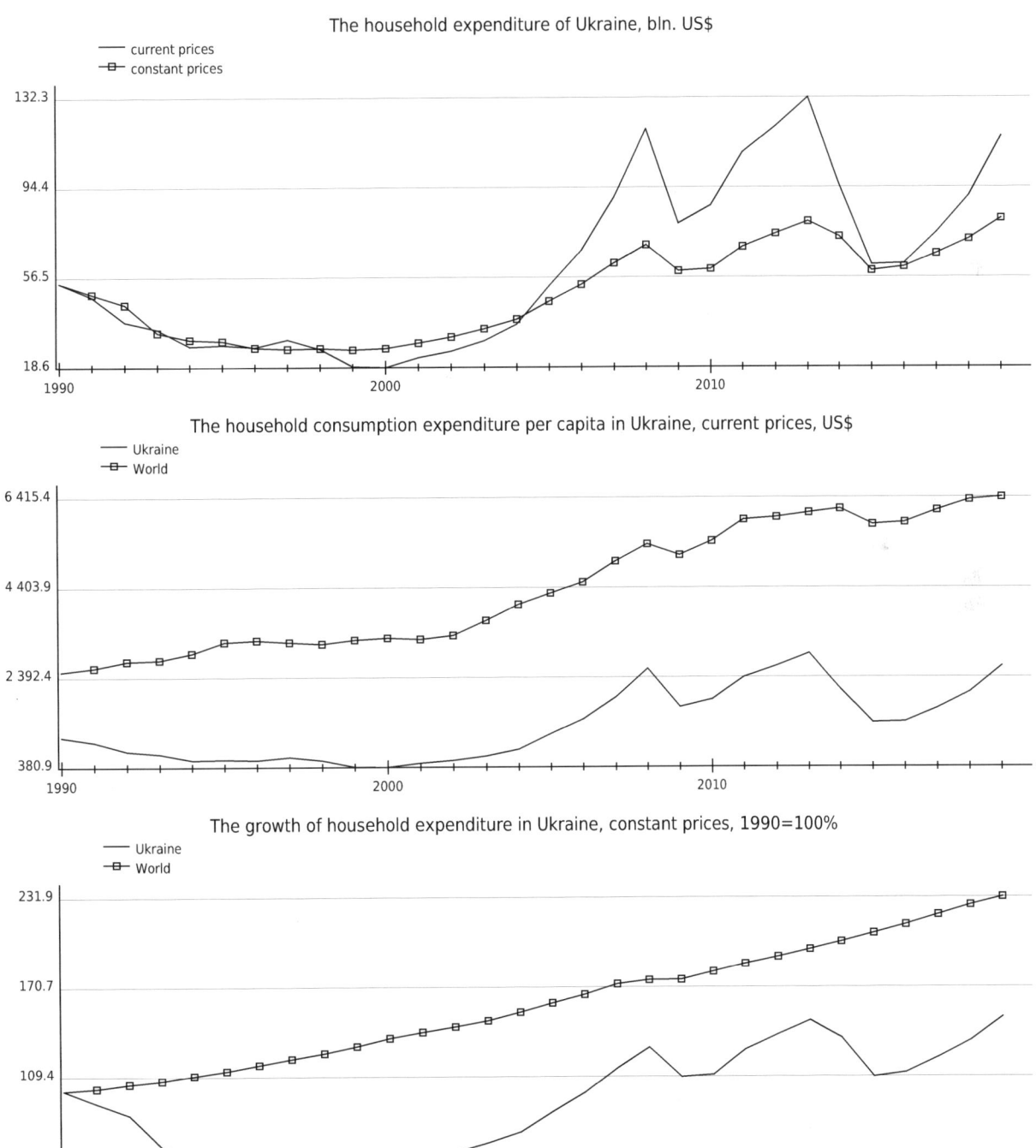

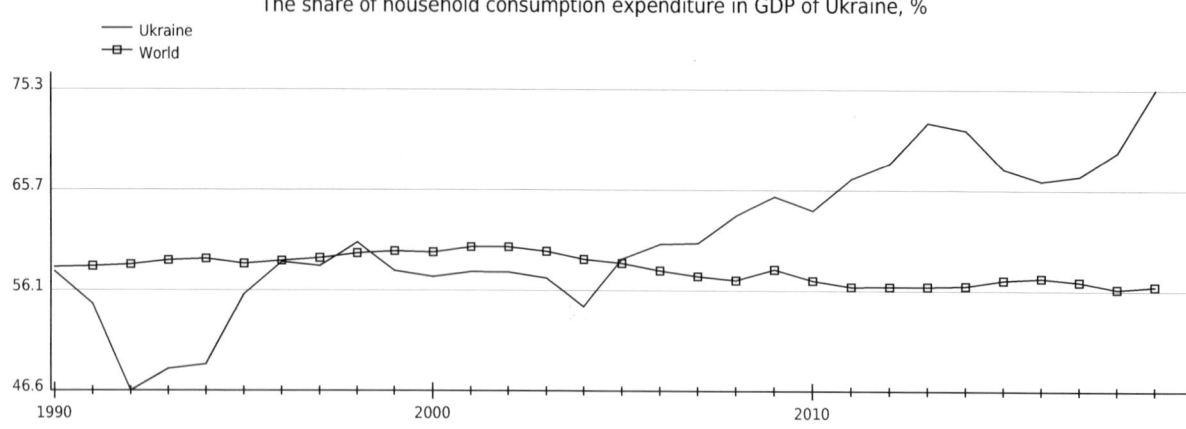

The share of household consumption expenditure in GDP of Ukraine, %

The 1990s

The Ukrainian household expenditure was $33.4 billion per year in the 1990s, ranked 45th in the world, and was on a par with the UAE ($33.5 billion), Peru ($32.8 billion). The share in the world was 0.20%, and 0.60% in Europe.

The share of household expenditure in GDP of Ukraine was 54.2% in the 1990s, ranked 161st in the world, and was on a par with Hungary (54.3%), Aruba (54.4%), San Marino (54.4%).

The Ukrainian household consumption expenditure per capita was $657.1 in the 1990s, ranked 141st in the world, and was on a par with South-Eastern Asia ($652.5), Papua New Guinea ($642.2). The household consumption expenditure per capita in Ukraine was less than household expenditure per capita in the world ($2 963.9) in 4.5 times, and was less than household consumption expenditure per capita in Europe ($7 702.2) in 11.7 times.

The growth of household consumption expenditure in Ukraine was -7.8% in the 1990s, ranked 198th in the world. The growth of household expenditure in Ukraine (-7.8%) was less than growth of household consumption expenditure in the world (3.0%), was less than growth of household expenditure in Europe (1.8%).

Comparison with neighbors. The Ukrainian household consumption expenditure was greater than in Romania ($23.5 billion), in Hungary ($23.5 billion), in Belarus ($9.0 billion), in Bulgaria ($8.2 billion), and in Moldova ($1.5 billion); but less than in Russia ($198.5 billion) and in Poland ($76.3 billion). The household expenditure per capita in Ukraine was greater than in Moldova ($342.8); but less than in Hungary ($2.3 thousand), in Poland ($1 987.8), in Russia ($1 342.0), in Romania ($1 022.4), in Bulgaria ($972.2), and in Belarus ($898.2). The growth of household expenditure in Ukraine was greater than in Moldova (-9.7%); but less than in Poland (3.2%), in Romania (0.17%), in Hungary (-0.024%), in Belarus (-0.89%), in Russia (-1.8%), and in Bulgaria (-4.3%).

Comparison with leaders. The Ukrainian household consumption expenditure was less than in the USA ($4.9 trillion), in Japan ($2.3 trillion), in Germany ($1.2 trillion), in the UK ($884.5 billion), and in France ($783.0 billion). The Ukraine's household consumption expenditure per capita was less than in the United States ($18.5 thousand), in Japan ($18.2 thousand), in the United Kingdom ($15.3 thousand), in Germany ($15.2 thousand), and in France ($13.2 thousand). The growth of household consumption expenditure in Ukraine was less than in the United States (3.4%), in the United Kingdom (2.8%), in Germany (2.1%), in Japan (1.8%), and in France (1.8%).

The 2000s

The household consumption expenditure of Ukraine was $54.2 billion per year in the 2000s, ranked 51st in the world, and was on a par with Singapore ($54.5 billion), Hungary ($55.1 billion). The share in the world was 0.20%, and 0.62% in Europe.

The share of household expenditure in GDP of Ukraine was 60.6% in the 2000s, ranked 127th in the world, and was on a par with Latvia (60.5%), Southern Africa (60.7%), the Solomon Islands (60.5%).

The household expenditure per capita in Ukraine was $1 148.9 in the 2000s, ranked 136th in the world. The household consumption expenditure per capita in Ukraine was less than household expenditure per capita in the world ($4 208.2) in 3.7 times, and was less than household expenditure per capita in Europe ($11 901.2) in 10.4 times.

The growth of household consumption expenditure in Ukraine was 8.5% in the 2000s, ranked 17th in the world, and was on a par with Afghanistan (8.5%), Russia (8.6%). The growth of household consumption expenditure in Ukraine (8.5%) was greater than growth of

Chapter XIII. Household consumption expenditure

household expenditure in the world (3.0%), was greater than growth of household consumption expenditure in Europe (2.0%).

Comparison with neighbors. The household consumption expenditure of Ukraine was greater than in Bulgaria ($20.4 billion), in Belarus ($17.0 billion), and in Moldova ($3.3 billion); but less than in Russia ($394.1 billion), in Poland ($194.0 billion), in Romania ($69.5 billion), and in Hungary ($55.1 billion). The Ukraine's household expenditure per capita was greater than in Moldova ($794.5); but less than in Hungary ($5.5 thousand), in Poland ($5.0 thousand), in Romania ($3.2 thousand), in Russia ($2.7 thousand), in Bulgaria ($2.6 thousand), and in Belarus ($1 763.2). The growth of household consumption expenditure in Ukraine was greater than in Moldova (7.8%), in Romania (7.7%), in Bulgaria (6.4%), in Poland (3.7%), and in Hungary (2.3%); but less than in Belarus (10.8%) and in Russia (8.6%).

Comparison with leaders. The household consumption expenditure of Ukraine was less than in the USA ($8.5 trillion), in Japan ($2.6 trillion), in Germany ($1.5 trillion), in the United Kingdom ($1.5 trillion), and in France ($1.1 trillion). The household consumption expenditure per capita in Ukraine was less than in the USA ($28.8 thousand), in the UK ($25.0 thousand), in Japan ($20.4 thousand), in Germany ($18.9 thousand), and in France ($18.1 thousand). The growth of household consumption expenditure in Ukraine was greater than in the United States (2.4%), in the UK (2.1%), in France (2.0%), in Japan (0.81%), and in Germany (0.46%).

The 2010s

The Ukrainian household expenditure was $94.9 billion per year in the 2010s, ranked 54th in the world. The share in the world was 0.22%, and 0.82% in Europe.

The share of household expenditure in GDP of Ukraine was 69.1% in the 2010s, ranked 82nd in the world, and was on a par with Laos (69.1%), Tunisia (69.2%), Greece (69.0%).

The Ukrainian household consumption expenditure per capita was $2 111.1 in the 2010s, ranked 139th in the world, and was on a par with Mongolia ($2.1 thousand), Indonesia ($2.1 thousand), Central Asia ($2.2 thousand). The Ukrainian household expenditure per capita was less than household consumption expenditure per capita in the world ($6 018.5) in 2.9 times, and was less than household consumption expenditure per capita in Europe ($15 614.2) in 7.4 times.

The growth of household expenditure in Ukraine was 3.2% in the 2010s, ranked 96th in the world, and was on a par with Zambia (3.2%). The growth of household consumption expenditure in Ukraine (3.2%) was greater than growth of household expenditure in the world (2.8%), was greater than growth of household expenditure in Europe (1.3%).

Comparison with neighbors. The Ukraine's household consumption expenditure was 33.2% higher than in Hungary ($71.3 billion), 2.7 times higher than in Bulgaria ($35.2 billion), 2.9 times higher than in Belarus ($32.6 billion), and 11.7 times higher than in Moldova ($8.1 billion); but 9.6 times lower than in Russia ($914.4 billion), 3.3 times lower than in Poland ($312.1 billion), and 23.7% lower than in Romania ($124.4 billion). The Ukraine's household consumption expenditure per capita was 5.6% higher than in Moldova ($1 998.9); but 3.9 times lower than in Poland ($8.2 thousand), 3.4 times lower than in Hungary ($7.3 thousand), 3.0 times lower than in Russia ($6.3 thousand), 3.0 times lower than in Romania ($6.2 thousand), 2.3 times lower than in Bulgaria ($4.9 thousand), and 39.0% lower than in Belarus ($3.5 thousand). The growth of household consumption expenditure in Ukraine was greater than in Poland (2.9%), in Bulgaria (2.8%), in Russia (2.4%), and in Hungary (2.2%); but less than in Belarus (4.7%), in Moldova (4.4%), and in Romania (4.0%).

Comparison with leaders. The Ukrainian household consumption expenditure was 128.4 times lower than in the United States ($12.2 trillion), 41.4 times lower than in China ($3.9 trillion), 31.5 times lower than in Japan ($3.0 trillion), 20.6 times lower than in Germany ($2.0 trillion), and 18.8 times lower than in the United Kingdom ($1.8 trillion). The household expenditure per capita in Ukraine was 18.1 times lower than in the USA ($38.2 thousand), 12.9 times lower than in the UK ($27.2 thousand), 11.3 times lower than in Germany ($23.9 thousand), 11.1 times lower than in Japan ($23.4 thousand), and 24.7% lower than in China ($2.8 thousand). The growth of household consumption expenditure in Ukraine was greater than in the USA (2.4%), in the UK (1.8%), in Germany (1.4%), and in Japan (0.64%); but less than in China (8.3%).

Chapter XIV. Food consumption

During the research period the food consumption grew in stimulants (in 4.4 times), alcoholic beverages (in 3.1 times), spices (in 2.3 times), eggs (by 73.8%), vegetables (by 72.8%), fruits (by 63.5%), fish (by 56.2%), vegetable oils (by 53.1%), meat (by 25.9%), sugar (by 17.1%), treenuts (by 14.8%), starchy roots (by 3.1%), but fell in milk (by 2.6%), cereals (by 18.1%), pulses (by 90.7%).

These are the correlation coefficients between the GNI per capita in constant prices and the food consumption: meat (0.984), fruits (0.858), eggs (0.741), vegetables (0.729), spices (0.72), treenuts (0.539), alcoholic beverages (0.531), starchy roots (0.373), stimulants (0.364), vegetable oils (0.353), fish (0.087), sugar (0.082), cereals (-0.717), pulses (-0.757), milk (-0.897).

The 1990s

Kcal supply in Ukraine was 2 967.3 kcal/capita/day in the 1990s, ranked 41st in the world, and was on a par with Mexico (2 984.9 kcal/capita/day), Lithuania (2 990.0 kcal/capita/day), Barbados (2 940.1 kcal/capita/day). Kcal supply in Ukraine was greater than in the world (2 652.6 kcal/capita/day), and was less than in Europe (3 214.0 kcal/capita/day). Structure of kcal supply: cereals (42.9%), sugar (13%), milk (8.6%), starchy roots (8.2%), vegetable oils (7%), and others (20.3%).

Protein supply in Ukraine was 84.5 g/capita/day in the 1990s, ranked 52nd in the world, and was on a par with Uruguay (84.5 g/capita/day), Barbados (84.9 g/capita/day), Western Asia (85.1 g/capita/day). Protein supply in Ukraine was greater than in the world (72.1 g/capita/day), and was less than in Europe (97.9 g/capita/day). Structure of protein supply: cereals (44.1%), milk (16.8%), meat (16.3%), starchy roots (6.9%), eggs (3.5%), and others (12.4%).

Fat supply in Ukraine was 77.1 g/capita/day in the 1990s, ranked 64th in the world, and was on a par with Ecuador (77.2 g/capita/day), Paraguay (77.0 g/capita/day), Western Asia (77.7 g/capita/day). Fat supply in Ukraine was greater than in the world (69.0 g/capita/day), and was less than in Europe (119.3 g/capita/day). Structure of fat supply: vegetable oils (30.3%), meat (20.7%), milk (18.1%), cereals (6%), eggs (3.6%), and others (21.3%).

These are the levels of food consumption in the world rankings: 23rd - starchy roots (132.3 kg/capita/yr), 32nd - cereals (165.6 kg/capita/yr), 35th - milk (158.7 kg/capita/yr), 38th - eggs (10.2 kg/capita/yr), 41st - sugar (40.5 kg/capita/yr), 43rd - vegetables (92.0 kg/capita/yr), 61st - treenuts (1.2 kg/capita/yr), 74th - meat (41.1 kg/capita/yr), 85th - alcoholic beverages (24.0 kg/capita/yr), 88th - vegetable oils (8.5 kg/capita/yr), 94th - fish (9.5 kg/capita/yr), 110th - pulses (3.0 kg/capita/yr), 132nd - fruits (33.4 kg/capita/yr), 136th - stimulants (0.63 kg/capita/yr), 138th - spices (0.089 kg/capita/yr).

The 2000s

Kcal supply in Ukraine was 3 135.4 kcal/capita/day in the 2000s, ranked 40th in the world, and was on a par with Russia (3 137.8 kcal/capita/day), Australasia (3 119.9 kcal/capita/day), Sweden (3 118.3 kcal/capita/day). Kcal supply in Ukraine was greater than in the world (2 765.9 kcal/capita/day), and was less than in Europe (3 316.3 kcal/capita/day). Structure of kcal supply: cereals (37.9%), sugar (14.3%), vegetable oils (9.4%), milk (8.7%), starchy roots (7.9%), and others (21.8%).

Protein supply in Ukraine was 86.4 g/capita/day in the 2000s, ranked 58th in the world, and was on a par with the Bahamas (86.7 g/capita/day), Lebanon (86.8 g/capita/day), Barbados (86.0 g/capita/day). Protein supply in Ukraine was greater than in the world (76.5 g/capita/day), and was less than in Europe (100.0 g/capita/day). Structure of protein supply: cereals (40%), milk (17.7%), meat (15.6%), starchy roots (6.9%), fish (5.3%), and others (14.5%).

Fat supply in Ukraine was 86.2 g/capita/day in the 2000s, ranked 67th in the world, and was on a par with Grenada (86.2 g/capita/day), Mauritius (86.4 g/capita/day), Saudi Arabia (85.5 g/capita/day). Fat supply in Ukraine was greater than in the world (76.9 g/capita/day), and was less than in Europe (123.9 g/capita/day). Structure of fat supply: vegetable oils (38.5%), milk (17.8%), meat (16.1%), cereals (5%), eggs (4.1%), and others (18.5%).

These are the levels of food consumption in the world rankings: 19th - sugar (48.3 kg/capita/yr), 21st - eggs (13.1 kg/capita/yr), 23rd - starchy roots (135.5 kg/capita/yr), 40th - vegetables (119.0 kg/capita/yr), 41st - milk (170.3 kg/capita/yr), 42nd - cereals (155.0 kg/capita/yr), 53rd - alcoholic beverages (55.8 kg/capita/yr), 66th - vegetable oils (12.2 kg/capita/yr), 78th - fish (15.4 kg/capita/yr), 81st - treenuts (1.3 kg/capita/yr), 91st - meat (38.8 kg/capita/yr), 98th - stimulants (2.3 kg/capita/yr), 119th - pulses (2.4 kg/capita/yr), 140th - spices (0.14 kg/capita/yr), 142nd - fruits (37.8 kg/capita/yr).

The 2010s

Chapter XIV. Food consumption

Kcal supply in Ukraine was 3 154.0 kcal/capita/day in the 2010s, ranked 47th in the world, and was on a par with Albania (3 146.3 kcal/capita/day), Sweden (3 164.3 kcal/capita/day), Latvia (3 141.5 kcal/capita/day). Kcal supply in Ukraine was greater than in the world (2 869.3 kcal/capita/day), and was less than in Europe (3 363.0 kcal/capita/day). Structure of kcal supply: cereals (34%), sugar (14%), vegetable oils (10%), milk (8%), starchy roots (7.9%), and others (26.1%).

Protein supply in Ukraine was 87.9 g/capita/day in the 2010s, ranked 61st in the world, and was on a par with Japan (87.8 g/capita/day), Oman (88.5 g/capita/day). Protein supply in Ukraine was greater than in the world (80.6 g/capita/day), and was less than in Europe (102.1 g/capita/day). Structure of protein supply: cereals (35.5%), meat (19.8%), milk (15.9%), starchy roots (6.8%), eggs (5.9%), and others (16.1%).

Fat supply in Ukraine was 91.8 g/capita/day in the 2010s, ranked 65th in the world, and was on a par with Estonia (91.5 g/capita/day), Mexico (92.1 g/capita/day), Mauritius (90.9 g/capita/day). Fat supply in Ukraine was greater than in the world (82.4 g/capita/day), and was less than in Europe (128.7 g/capita/day). Structure of fat supply: vegetable oils (38.7%), meat (18.3%), milk (15.8%), eggs (5.2%), cereals (4.3%), and others (17.7%).

These are the levels of food consumption in the world rankings: 4th - eggs (17.7 kg/capita/yr), 21st - starchy roots (136.4 kg/capita/yr), 23rd - vegetables (159.0 kg/capita/yr), 26th - sugar (47.4 kg/capita/yr), 42nd - alcoholic beverages (74.7 kg/capita/yr), 49th - milk (154.8 kg/capita/yr), 64th - vegetable oils (13.0 kg/capita/yr), 66th - cereals (140.2 kg/capita/yr), 82nd - meat (51.7 kg/capita/yr), 84th - fish (14.8 kg/capita/yr), 87th - treenuts (1.4 kg/capita/yr), 101st - stimulants (2.8 kg/capita/yr), 126th - fruits (54.7 kg/capita/yr), 132nd - spices (0.21 kg/capita/yr), 139th - pulses (1.6 kg/capita/yr).

Part V. Reproduction

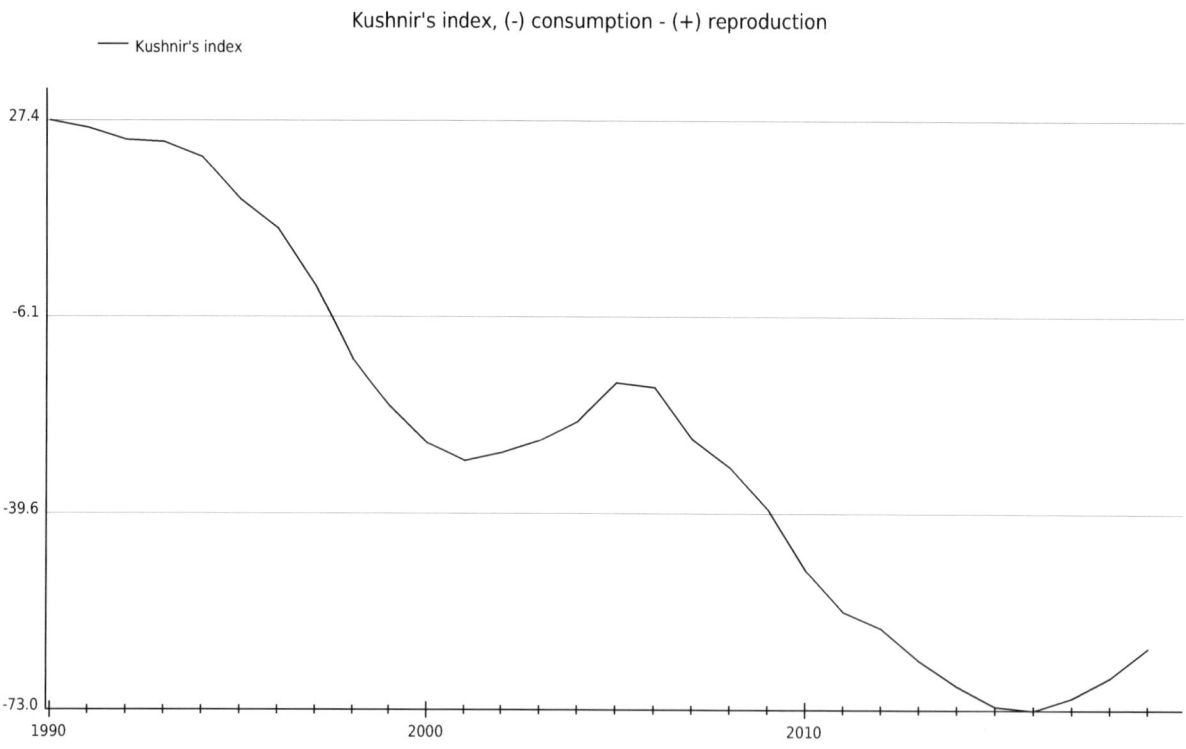

Chapter XV. Gross fixed capital formation

(including Acquisitions less disposals of valuables)

The fixed capital formation of Ukraine grew up from $14.2 billion per year in the 1990s to $23.1 billion per year in the 2010s, that is by $8.9 billion or 62.8%. The change occurred at $15.8 billion due to a 3.2-fold increase in prices, as also at -$5.2 billion due to a 1.7-fold decrease in per capita rate, as well as at -$1.6 billion due to the drop in population. The average annual growth in fixed capital formation is -4.4%. The minimum value of gross fixed capital formation was in 1999 at $6.4 billion. The maximum value of gross fixed capital formation was in 2008 at $48.8 billion.

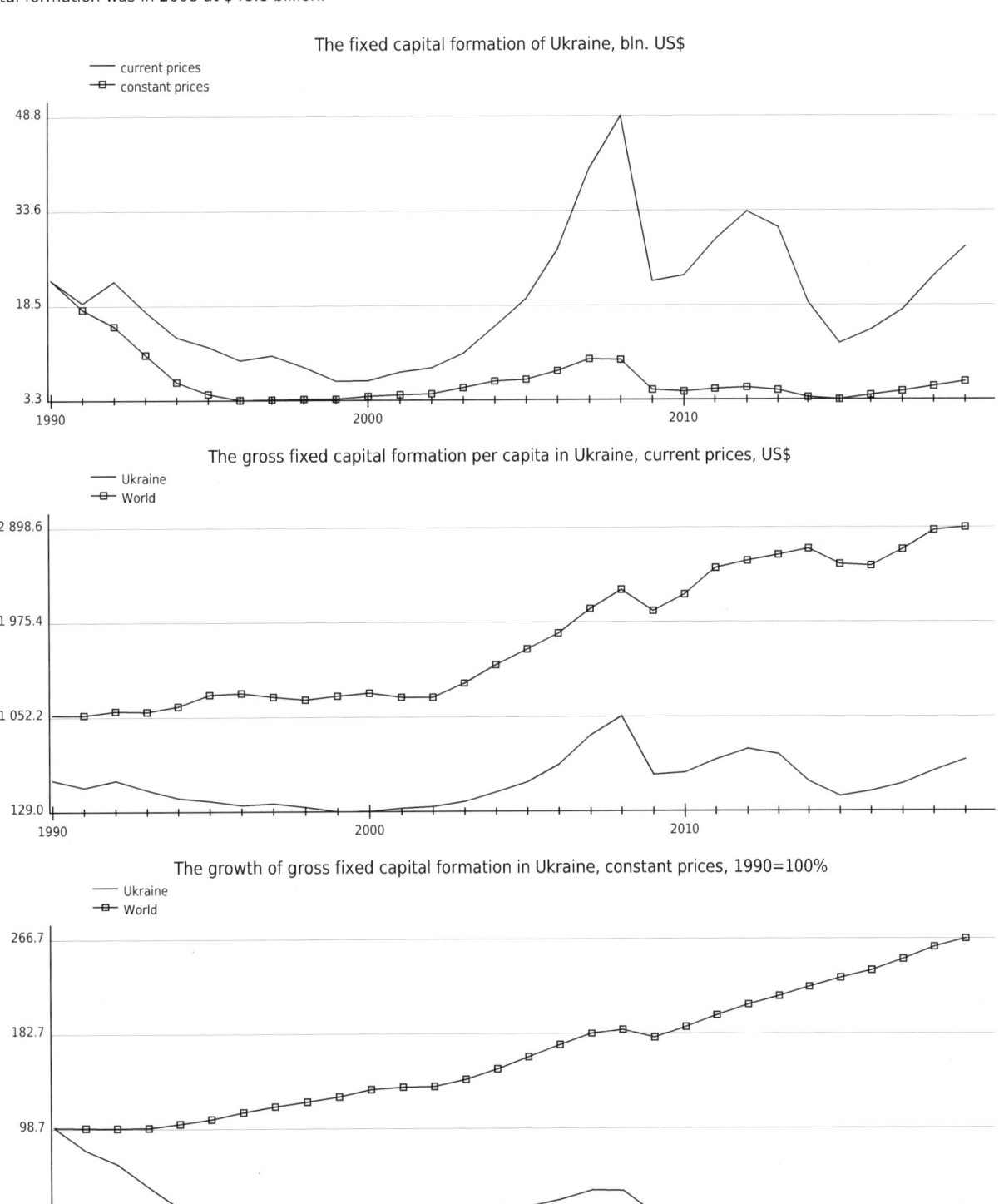

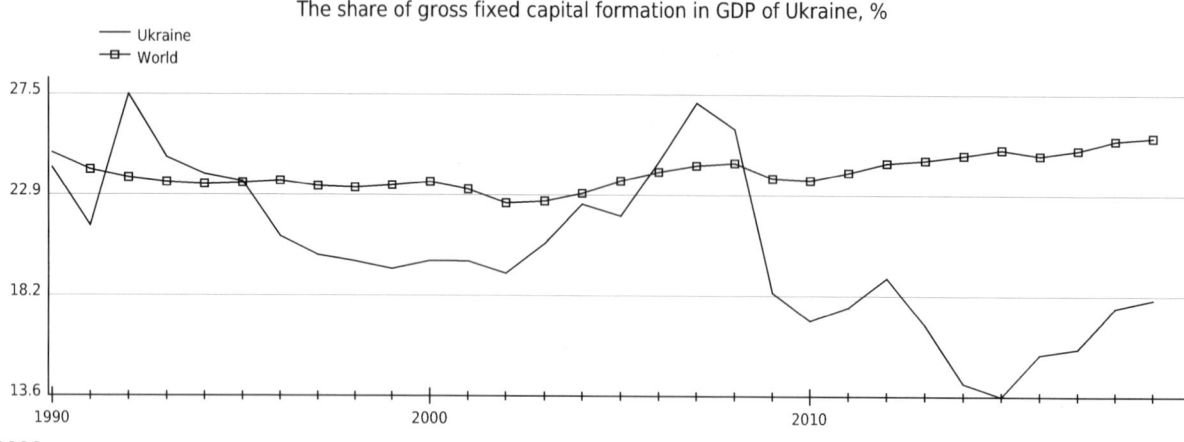

The 1990s

The gross fixed capital formation of Ukraine was $14.2 billion per year in the 1990s, ranked 45th in the world. The share in the world was 0.21%, and 0.66% in Europe.

The share of gross fixed capital formation in GDP of Ukraine was 23.0% in the 1990s, ranked 86th in the world, and was on a par with Bahrain (23.0%), Western Europe (23.0%), Andorra (23.0%).

The fixed capital formation per capita in Ukraine was $279.2 in the 1990s, ranked 129th in the world, and was on a par with Bosnia and Herzegovina ($281.6), Mauritania ($273.4). The fixed capital formation per capita in Ukraine was less than fixed capital formation per capita in the world ($1 183.8) in 4.2 times, and was less than gross fixed capital formation per capita in Europe ($2 956.1) in 10.6 times.

The growth of gross fixed capital formation in Ukraine was -18.7% in the 1990s, ranked 207th in the world. The growth of gross fixed capital formation in Ukraine (-18.7%) was less than growth of fixed capital formation in the world (2.8%), was less than growth of fixed capital formation in Europe (0.024%).

Comparison with neighbors. The Ukrainian fixed capital formation was greater than in Hungary ($9.9 billion), in Romania ($6.7 billion), in Belarus ($4.2 billion), in Bulgaria ($1.8 billion), and in Moldova ($497.6 million); but less than in Russia ($98.2 billion) and in Poland ($25.0 billion). The gross fixed capital formation per capita in Ukraine was greater than in Bulgaria ($215.9) and in Moldova ($115.0); but less than in Hungary ($953.2), in Russia ($664.1), in Poland ($652.8), in Belarus ($414.1), and in Romania ($291.9). The growth of fixed capital formation in Ukraine was less than in Poland (7.4%), in Hungary (2.0%), in Bulgaria (-0.26%), in Romania (-3.7%), in Belarus (-5.6%), in Moldova (-16.0%), and in Russia (-17.9%).

Comparison with leaders. The fixed capital formation of Ukraine was less than in the United States ($1.6 trillion), in Japan ($1.3 trillion), in Germany ($520.7 billion), in France ($299.3 billion), and in the UK ($250.0 billion). The Ukrainian gross fixed capital formation per capita was less than in Japan ($10.4 thousand), in Germany ($6.5 thousand), in the USA ($6.1 thousand), in France ($5.0 thousand), and in the United Kingdom ($4.3 thousand). The growth of fixed capital formation in Ukraine was less than in the USA (4.8%), in Germany (2.4%), in the United Kingdom (1.7%), in France (1.5%), and in Japan (0.18%).

The 2000s

The fixed capital formation of Ukraine was $20.7 billion per year in the 2000s, ranked 50th in the world, and was on a par with Egypt ($20.5 billion). The share in the world was 0.19%, and 0.62% in Europe.

The share of fixed capital formation in GDP of Ukraine was 23.1% in the 2000s, ranked 103rd in the world, and was on a par with Georgia (23.1%), Macao (23.1%), the Marshall Islands (23.1%).

The Ukraine's fixed capital formation per capita was $438.3 in the 2000s, ranked 137th in the world, and was on a par with South-Eastern Asia ($439.7), Paraguay ($440.8), Mongolia ($434.4). The fixed capital formation per capita in Ukraine was less than fixed capital formation per capita in the world ($1 690.7) in 3.9 times, and was less than fixed capital formation per capita in Europe ($4 590.9) in 10.5 times.

The growth of fixed capital formation in Ukraine was 3.4% in the 2000s, ranked 123rd in the world, and was on a par with the Philippines (3.4%). The growth of fixed capital formation in Ukraine (3.4%) was less than growth of gross fixed capital formation in the

Chapter XV. Gross fixed capital formation

world (3.5%), was greater than growth of fixed capital formation in Europe (1.6%).

Comparison with neighbors. The Ukrainian fixed capital formation was greater than in Belarus ($9.2 billion), in Bulgaria ($8.0 billion), and in Moldova ($971.0 million); but less than in Russia ($172.9 billion), in Poland ($64.5 billion), in Romania ($29.9 billion), and in Hungary ($24.2 billion). The Ukraine's fixed capital formation per capita was greater than in Moldova ($233.6); but less than in Hungary ($2.4 thousand), in Poland ($1 678.5), in Romania ($1 392.3), in Russia ($1 198.4), in Bulgaria ($1 033.7), and in Belarus ($955.6). The growth of gross fixed capital formation in Ukraine was greater than in Hungary (2.5%); but less than in Belarus (13.9%), in Bulgaria (12.2%), in Russia (10.0%), in Romania (9.7%), in Moldova (6.0%), and in Poland (3.9%).

Comparison with leaders. The fixed capital formation of Ukraine was less than in the USA ($2.8 trillion), in Japan ($1.2 trillion), in China ($1.0 trillion), in Germany ($557.7 billion), and in France ($463.9 billion). The Ukraine's gross fixed capital formation per capita was less than in the USA ($9.4 thousand), in Japan ($9.0 thousand), in France ($7.4 thousand), in Germany ($6.9 thousand), and in China ($782.2). The growth of gross fixed capital formation in Ukraine was greater than in France (1.6%), in the USA (0.43%), in Germany (-0.56%), and in Japan (-2.0%); but less than in China (13.4%).

The 2010s

The Ukraine's gross fixed capital formation was $23.1 billion per year in the 2010s, ranked 62nd in the world. The share in the world was 0.12%, and 0.54% in Europe.

The share of fixed capital formation in GDP of Ukraine was 16.8% in the 2010s, ranked 181st in the world, and was on a par with Yemen (16.8%), Macao (16.9%), the United Kingdom (16.9%).

The Ukrainian gross fixed capital formation per capita was $513.3 in the 2010s, ranked 158th in the world, and was on a par with Swaziland ($513.3), Vietnam ($515.2), Southern Asia ($516.4). The fixed capital formation per capita in Ukraine was less than fixed capital formation per capita in the world ($2 621.1) in 5.1 times, and was less than gross fixed capital formation per capita in Europe ($5 775.6) in 11.3 times.

The growth of gross fixed capital formation in Ukraine was 2.3% in the 2010s, ranked 121st in the world, and was on a par with Western Europe (2.4%). The growth of fixed capital formation in Ukraine (2.3%) was less than growth of fixed capital formation in the world (4.1%), was greater than growth of fixed capital formation in Europe (2.2%).

Comparison with neighbors. The Ukrainian fixed capital formation was 17.1% higher than in Belarus ($19.7 billion), 2.0 times higher than in Bulgaria ($11.5 billion), and 10.5 times higher than in Moldova ($2.2 billion); but 16.5 times lower than in Russia ($380.9 billion), 4.3 times lower than in Poland ($100.2 billion), 2.1 times lower than in Romania ($48.1 billion), and 25.3% lower than in Hungary ($30.9 billion). The fixed capital formation per capita in Ukraine was 6.1 times lower than in Hungary ($3.2 thousand), 5.1 times lower than in Poland ($2.6 thousand), 5.1 times lower than in Russia ($2.6 thousand), 4.7 times lower than in Romania ($2.4 thousand), 4.1 times lower than in Belarus ($2.1 thousand), 3.1 times lower than in Bulgaria ($1 590.4), and 4.7% lower than in Moldova ($538.3). The growth of gross fixed capital formation in Ukraine was greater than in Russia (1.5%), in Belarus (0.78%), and in Bulgaria (-1.2%); but less than in Moldova (8.0%), in Hungary (4.6%), in Poland (3.3%), and in Romania (3.0%).

Comparison with leaders. The Ukrainian gross fixed capital formation was 196.0 times lower than in China ($4.5 trillion), 156.0 times lower than in the USA ($3.6 trillion), 52.4 times lower than in Japan ($1.2 trillion), 32.6 times lower than in Germany ($752.5 billion), and 30.2 times lower than in India ($696.8 billion). The fixed capital formation per capita in Ukraine was 21.9 times lower than in the United States ($11.3 thousand), 18.4 times lower than in Japan ($9.5 thousand), 17.9 times lower than in Germany ($9.2 thousand), 6.3 times lower than in China ($3.2 thousand), and 4.1% lower than in India ($535.2). The growth of fixed capital formation in Ukraine was greater than in Japan (1.8%); but less than in China (8.0%), in India (5.8%), in the United States (3.8%), and in Germany (2.8%).

Made in United States
Orlando, FL
17 January 2023